Best Wishes

GEORDIE ARMSTRONG
ON THE WING

Published by
Legends Publishing

E-mail david@legendspublishing.net
Website www.legendspublishing.net

Copyright 2014

**This book is dedicated to George Armstrong's five granchildren:
George, Jude, Cody, Mya and Karl**

The photographs featured in this book have been sourced from the Armstrong family's personal collection. We would also like to thank the staff at Colorsport and MirrorPix for their generous help. It has unfortunately not been possible to trace every photographer, however, we'd delighted to add credits in subsequent updates if new information becomes available.

CONTENTS

PREFACE

George Armstrong, as you will learn in the pages that follow, was the antithesis of the modern day football superstar – yet to those who knew him, played with him and cheered him on from the terraces – he was just that... a bona fide Arsenal Superstar.

The words 'Great' and 'Legend' are bandied about very readily in a modern era, in which television, as well as written and social media, scrutinizes every aspect of a top footballer's life, and there have been many Arsenal players labelled with monumental superlatives whose actual 'greatness' could be seriously questioned – but this book is inspired by one where there is no debate.

George 'Geordie' Armstrong served Arsenal Football club for 27 years, during spells as both a player and a coach, but in a tragic twist of fate, he was cruelly taken from his family and his club at just 56 years of age. On October 31, 2000, George was working on the training pitch at London Colney with his Arsenal reserves when he suddenly collapsed, having suffered a brain haemorrhage, from which he never recovered.

4

No family would ever wish to lose such a loved husband and father, but there is acknowledgement within Geordie's family that if he could have chosen when and where to leave us, then it would have been on a training pitch, at Arsenal, with his 'lads'. But from that tragedy was born a desire to somehow build a record of what Geordie had meant to so many people, and indeed how much he'd accomplished in the game, so that future generations of the Armstrong family, as well as future Arsenal fans, would understand what George Armstrong had achieved as a footballer.

The original, and biggest driver behind this homage to Geordie, has been his daughter, Jill. When her father passed away 14 years ago, she started to collect the memories of her dad's ex-team mates and from Arsenal fans, all of whom were invited to write about their recollections of her father. At the time her brother Tom and his fiancé were expecting their first child, and it was the realisation that future grandchildren would never know their grand-father, that instilled Jill with a sense of purpose.

But, despite receiving over 600 letters from Arsenal supporters, team mates and coaching colleagues, taking things to the next stage became too personal and emotionally difficult for Jill, meaning the correspondence, newspaper cuttings and tributes remained treasured, unshared mementoes.

However, it was thanks to Jill's introduction to social media via Twitter, prompted by a trip to her father's memorial pitch at Colney with her own children, that rekindled the desire to share her father's memory once more, and as a keen Arsenal Blogger, I was humbled when Jill approached me to assist her with this very personal project. I am proud to have written this book and have tried my upmost to capture the essence of George Armstrong.

In writing this book I have chosen not to follow the conventional 'biography' route but, instead, attempted to tell the story of Geordie Armstrong with the assistance of those who knew him most. To build a picture of the man using the memories and recollections of those who loved him; those who called him their friend; those who played with him on football pitches all over the world; and those coached by him. Sharing his wisdom with the assistance of Arsene Wenger and Don Howe, iconic players such as Dennis Bergkamp, Frank McLintock, Liam Brady and Bob Wilson, as well as the great and the good that span Geordie's whole football career, has been a wonderful journey for me personally too.

I hope that younger Arsenal supporters will read this book, alongside the 'more senior' diehard Gunners who saw him play week in, week out – for there are many figures that have shaped the history, tradition and heritage of Arsenal Football Club – and the memories that follow leave little doubt that George Armstrong is amongst the most significant in the past half century.

Dave Seager

FOREWORD

My father lived and breathed football. It was his life, and ours, for so long. Dad would have felt embarrassed by 'all this fuss', as he would have put it. But secretly, I think he would have been chuffed! To say what dad meant to my mum, brother Tom and I would be impossible. There are not enough pages in this book to fill it with the love mum, Tom and I had for dad.

Tom's first child was on its way when my dad passed, (my parent's first grandchild) and I felt the need to create a book of peoples' memories about dad for the future grandchildren, of which there are five – George, Jude, Cody, Mya and Karl. I wanted them to have a book that they could read one day, and learn about their grandfather and hear from the people that knew him best – fellow players and Arsenal fans. After the funeral I started writing to people – players, fans and friends – however, the grief kicked in and I stopped. Eventually, many years later, I picked up the book project idea again – largely thanks to social media.

In November 2013, after the 13th anniversary of dad's passing, I started tweeting photos of dad. The response I experienced was amazing. The Arsenal fans were wonderful and I developed some great correspondence with a few supporters. I felt the overwhelming need to finish dad's book, and I wanted a supporter to write it. Dave Seager came highly recommended and I'd like to thank Peter Nelson for the introduction. Dave and I clicked instantly and I knew he was the perfect man to write the book

about my father. In my view Dave has managed to create the impossible, by bringing my father back to life. The way in which he has captured the pure essence of my father is incredible. A very talented writer, who has researched every angle of this publication and persevered, through thick and thin, to contact as many people as possible with a link to dad's life in football. I thank you Dave, as well as all the people who have contributed to this fantastic read.

Fans old and young can enjoy and learn about the man that was "Geordie Armstrong on the Wing" – someone I feel was part of the fabric that makes this "Great Club Great".

Jill Armstrong

INTRODUCTION

When I first arrived at Highbury in 1963 I was nervous, lonely and a little apprehensive. Not simply wondering if I would be good enough to play for the Arsenal, but whether the other players would look on me as a university lad. I needn't have worried because George Armstrong wouldn't have cared less if I'd been born into royalty. From the first day of my knowing Geordie, to the sad last day, he always had a word and a smile for me. I grew to love him like a brother, but then our special team in the late Sixties and early Seventies was like a band of brothers – one for all and all for one!

Within the group there were naturally a few who found training, travelling and, even playing, an occasional chore – but happily there were also those who never let the lazy ones get away with it – Geordie was the prime mover. Watching him in training or in competition, he was Mr. Perpetual Motion. No one was ever going to be able to accuse Geordie of giving anything other than 110%.

He was truly a great player, one who was somehow overlooked at international level by managers and coaches who should have known better. Better still to being a great player, he was a great human being. Generous, friendly and wonderfully humble.

Miami Beach boys in 1972

In my 12 years at Arsenal we did share a room occasionally, times that also remain treasured memories. In those moments we would talk about family and their importance – how proud he was of Marj, Tom and Jill – and how he loved them. Hopefully, Geordie recognised just how much we all loved him too. We were all proud to be his team mates and I am certain we will all continue to think about him, and the times we all spent together, until the day we will be reunited.

Thank you George Armstrong for enriching my life and the lives of all those you touched. With love.

Bob Wilson

GIVING GEORDIE SOME CONTEXT

The bare facts will inform us that George Armstrong, in a 16-year period spanning 1961 to 1977, appeared in the first team for Arsenal on no fewer than 621 occasions. For many years this made him Arsenal's record appearance holder – a feat only surpassed in recent years by David O'Leary, an old team mate of Geordie's and, latterly, Tony Adams. There should be no question that these represent three of the the greatest names in Arsenal post war history and, with modern players staying at one club the exception rather than the norm, it seems highly unlikely that these records will ever be surpassed.

I am certainly not intent on playing down the achievements of the above-mentioned legends one iota, but this book is a tribute to Geordie Armstrong – therefore I feel some context would be beneficial and I hope to simultaneously whet your appetite for more detail about this incredible man.

Of the 621 games in which George appeared for the Gunners, he started 607 of them, and was hardly ever substituted in an era when, with the exception of European nights, there was only one replacement, who wore the trusty number 12 shirt on the bench. So for virtually the whole of time as a player for the Arsenal Geordie was playing the full 90 minutes every time he pulled on the shirt.

Clubs since 1986/87 were able to use two substitutes in the League Cup and FA Cup and the Premier League the following season. In 1995/96 it became three from five named and now it is three from seven. Suffice to say 600-plus appearances in the 1990s and beyond is not necessarily on a par with a similar number in the 60s and 70s.

In addition, as you will increasingly understand as you read this book and see the photos, the pitches that Geordie Armstrong graced for Arsenal bear little resemblance to the surfaces on which O'Leary, in the latter half of his time at the top, and Adams, for his whole career, plied their trade. Geordie played for 16 seasons as a dynamic, wide player who covered more ground than any of his teammates, as they will tell you and, for at least four months of each season, on surfaces more akin to a farmer's field than the plush green carpets that have marked the Premier League era.

To illustrate my point, in 2014, I could suggest Liverpool's Stephen Gerrard as a similar example of a true one-club legend. As I write Gerrard has gone through the 600 barrier for Liverpool, but of those, in almost 60 he came off the bench and, in almost 100, he was substituted. So Gerrard has played 90 minutes on about 450 occasions compared to Geordie's 600-plus – that's the equivalent of 225 extra hours of top-flight football.

To make a meaningful comparison to the modern Arsenal era, it would be useful to look at our current longest serving regular first teamer. To the end of 2012/13, Theo Walcott, in seven seasons as a first teamer, has made a total of 276 appearances – however, 97 of those have been from the bench and, in over a third he did start, he failed to conclude the 90 minutes. I hope this brings a sense of clarity to Geordie's record of 621 games and the era in which he played.

Rarely injured, Geordie was pretty much a first choice player for Arsenal from 1963, through to his sale to Leicester in 1977, and in the four seasons between 1964 and 1968, he missed just five League matches. Geordie was ever-present in 1967/68.

George Armstrong made his debut on the 24 February 1962, away at Blackpool. At that time only one player in the club's history had made his league debut at a younger age. George was the ripe old age of 17 years and

Geordie's home debut in 1962

199 days and, to this day, only nine players have taken their League bow at a younger age. Not surprisingly, three are mentioned above.

Geordie joined a club who'd failed to win a trophy since clinching the title in 1953, but he was to become part of a side that would reach a Cup Final in five successive seasons between 1968 and 1972. Sadly, he was on the losing side in two League Cup finals, in 1968 and 1969, but real glory was lurking just around the corner.

Before I mention the success that was to come, it is worth bearing in mind that Armstrong was the only player to have survived through to 1970 from his debut season in 1961/62. In short he had given his all and remained loyal to his Arsenal for nine years before he first tasted glory – no other player could say as much at that time. But all that cumulative frustration was about to come to an epic end.

Geordie played in both legs of a hard fought European Fairs Cup clash with Anderlecht, helping overcome a 3-1 first leg away deficit to a then mighty Belgian side thanks to a 3-0 win back at Highbury – I cannot find any record of an award being given – but all those I have spoken to in the course of the research for this book, have told me that a certain, wee, Geordie Armstrong was everywhere that glorious muddy night under the North London floodlights. At the end of the season that saw his beloved Arsenal break their barren spell, Geordie Armstrong was voted the Supporters' Club Player of the Year for 1970, which demonstrates the respect the fans had for the player and due recognition of his unwavering loyalty.

For obvious reasons, the 1970/71 season will forever be enshrined within the hearts of Arsenal supporters and in the history of the football club – Arsenal claimed their first domestic League and FA Cup double, a feat only one team had done that century. The fact that it had been Arsenal's greatest rivals Spurs' exclusive boast from 1961 made the landmark achievement all the sweeter for everyone connected to the Gunners.

It was an incredible season – Arsenal played 64 matches in all competitions, including a good run in Europe and three rounds of the League Cup. George Armstrong played in virtually every minute of every one of the 64 games, missing only 50 minutes in total. No other outfield team member could boast the same service – the only other player to equal this achievement being the talismanic keeper, Bob Wilson.

This is quite simply a sensational record, given the pressure of going for the domestic double, the nature of the pitches and the lack of rest. To again put Geordie's achievement into perspective, when Arsenal next did the double, in 1997/98, not a single player was ever-present in the League and the most appearances by any one individual was from Nigel Winterburn who notched 49 across all competitions.

In that momentous 1970/71 campaign it took Arsenal 51 games to secure the League and the FA Cup, using a grand total of 16 players in the

Box-to-box in the mud

entire season – with only 14 playing more than 5 matches. Compare that to Wenger's doubles in 1997/98 – 21 players appeared 5 times or more times in the Premier League or FA Cup, and in 2001/02, that number had risen to 24.

The best box to box midfielders in the Premiership run between seven to eight miles per match and, against Inter Milan in January 2004, Freddie Ljungberg was recorded by Nike using GPS as running 9.4 miles in the 90 minutes. George Armstrong, in his era, was the equivalent of the great Swede in Wenger's winning sides, but produced that kind of workman-like performance over a far greater period.

Another of Geordie's modern Arsenal comparables would be Santi Cazorla, a player who plies his trade on the left flank, and is being asked to work box-to-box as Geordie did. Cazorla, in his first season in English football, featured impressively in every Premier League fixture, starting all bar one, and completed a grand total of 4,254 minutes in an Arsenal shirt. He appeared in 49 matches in total. Armstrong, in the Double season, played a total of 5710 minutes with no respite, a staggering 34% more football in far inferior conditions.

To balance this we must of course recognise that there is a much greater intensity and speed to the game then there was 40 years ago and, in some senses, it is not fair to compare 1971 an 2014. Players today are moving at greater speeds and in intense short bursts. However, even if the general pace of football was slower in the 1960s and early 70s, Geordie Armstrong did not reflect the norm – he undoubtedly played like a modern winger – making his achievements so remarkable.

Add into the melting pot the physical factor, particularly for a winger, as I was reminded by Frank McLintock: "Would the wingers of today have had the mental toughness Geordie had to have continually got up after being kicked repeatedly by the likes of Norman Hunter, Chopper Harris and numerous others I could name? I very much doubt it!"

I hope the more you recollect, delight in, or are discovering for the first time about Geordie Armstrong and how he played the game, the more you will grasp the significance and context I may appear to be labouring in this chapter. In short, they don't make too many like Geordie these days!

TO START AT THE END: A FITTING SEND OFF

"The world has lost a diamond of a fellow. This has shattered me because I honestly do not remember George having a days illness all the time I knew him. If he ever had to miss an Arsenal game through injury he was absolutely heartbroken. He lived for the game, but was a great family man as well."

Frank McLintock

Wednesday November 8, 2000, was the day that Arsenal Football Club shut down, pausing to honour, grieve and say farewell to one of its own – George 'Geordie' Armstrong. The funeral had been delayed, primarily because his death was so sudden there had been a post-mortem, but in addition to that, Geordie was also an organ donor. However, the memorial also had to fit in around Arsenal games, which may sound a little impersonal, but the reality was, in fact, very different – as events transpired.

In the days that followed Geordie's passing several people at Arsenal had phoned Marj, Geordie's widow, to offer their condolences and to offer their support by wishing to attend the funeral – Liam Brady also asked whether the family would mind if staff from the club could come to pay their respects too? The answer was an obviously yes as the family knew that Geordie never turned anyone away.

Arsenal then issued a memo to all the staff – a smaller and closer-knit club at the time – with virtually every employee confirming they wanted to be there to pay their respects. Every person in every department within

Highbury knew and loved Geordie – and they all wanted to say goodbye in person. Why? Because Geordie had made it his business to know all of them, with some individuals having been there since he arrived in the Sixties.

The unprecedented decision was therefore taken to close Arsenal Football Club for the day and three coaches were booked to bring the first team, the reserves, the youth side and all club staff. The groundsmen, the club shop assistants, the box office crew and the catering staff set off to pay their last respects with the flag above Highbury flying at half-mast in honour of an unquestionable legend of The Arsenal. The club also organised all the catering back at the Armstrong's house after the funeral, which was primarily for family, close friends and teammates from the 1971 Double winning team.

Geordie's body was finally released to the funeral directors' the night before the memorial and his family went to see him. Jill admits that she found it too difficult – her father looked so different after the work needed to remove his organs, but the family knew his loss had helped save other's lives. But the fact remains, when you are used to seeing a loved one so full of life and as vibrant as her father was, it is an unforgettably painful and raw experience. Tom, Geordie's son, stayed with Marj, advising her to concentrate on a feature she knew well – and she kissed him goodbye on the forehead. It was an emotionally draining, horrible experience, but they were able to return to the house comforted by their strong family bond and surrounded by the beautiful flowers that had been arriving all week.

The answer machine had been working over time – continually recording calls from family, friends and the players Geordie had coached – not to mention from Arsenal fans who had felt the loss profoundly too. There had been such an outpouring of emotion from others, but for Jill and the family, the numb feeling from the shock remained overpowering and she recalls that both she and her mother had literally shaken for a whole week. The doctor advised them it was natural – the body's way of dealing with the traumatic sequence of events – which had began on October 31 with the call from the Colney training ground to say that Geordie had suffered a massive haemorrhage at the brain stem.

Whilst the ambulance was taking Geordie from Colney to Hemel Hempstead Hospital, followed by Gary Lewin, who had tried so hard to keep him alive, the family rushed down from Cambridge. The call from Arsenal was taken at 4pm, and by 6pm, the family were by his side in hospital.

Before setting off, Tom had been asked to call Gary Lewin, who warned him about the severity of the situation, and that things were not looking positive. The Arsenal physio also informed him that his dad had stopped breathing and that he'd had to resuscitate him. Tom elected not to say anything about that conversation to his mum or Jill on the journey as he didn't want to worry them further – and hoped that, by the time they arrived at the hospital, everything would be alright. Sadly, that was not to be the case. When the family arrived they were shocked to find him in the corner of a small ward, cordoned off with simple curtains rather than a private room – the lack of privacy at this horrendous time was difficult for the family to take.

Geordie, as you will discover, had spent a lifetime trying to help others, and why should he be any different in death? So, when asked by the medical staff about Geordie carrying a donor card, the family agreed to them being taken instantly and without hesitation. In fact, knowing that other people would have their lives saved or extended made things a little easier, even rewarding. It was also what Geordie would have wanted.

As a Catholic the family knew Geordie would have also wanted his last rites read. Although he had never spoken about his wishes when he died in any detail – it had been mentioned in passing, so the hospital was asked to facilitate. The family all held hands with the priest and, according to Jill, the experience was strangely comforting and felt somehow right. It seemed so hard to accept that it was real. Shortly afterwards, at 10.10pm, George Armstrong was declared dead.

Jill remembers arriving home in the early hours, and even though she was mentally and physically drained, not wanting to go to bed – she says she felt that if she slept, she would wake up and it would all be real – if she stayed awake then, somehow, reality would continue to be put on hold.

For those that have been in that situation, you will recognise that, almost immediately, various events take over and plans have to be made. The family went to meet Father Tony Rogers at the local church. Both Geordie and Jill were 'occasional' practising Catholics and Marj, although not at the time, has since converted. Geordie did not believe in everything involved in the Catholic faith, but he took what he felt was right from his faith and loved the tradition and institution the Church provided. Jill laughed when she brought to mind a Christmas a few years earlier, when she attended mass with her dad, during which Geordie had sung at the top of his voice next to her. "He had such an awful voice, although I sounded as bad as he did, but I would mime or sing quietly rather than let anyone hear me. Dad didn't care who heard him though and said "God does not care what I sound like when I am in church!"

Marj, Jill and Tom found they agreed on pretty much everything when it came to the planning, which included requests to be made of Frank McLintock to tell a few stories and share memories, and for Bob Wilson to do a reading as both were amongst Geordie's oldest and dearest friends. The family also knew they were proud men and would find it extremely difficult to speak publicly in such emotional circumstances.

When registering the death, the three had gone together and, on arrival at the registrar's, were informed that only two people would be allowed in. To resolve the situation Jill had offered to stay outside, but Marj stood firm, stating in no uncertain terms that: "Their father has just died and you are

asking me to choose between my two children, you can forget it!" Thankfully, the registrar relented when he realised whose death he was recording and apparently became quite animated and insisted on writing Geordie's profession as 'Footballer' rather than 'Football Coach' as the family had suggested – the registrar chided them; "he may well have been a coach when he passed away, but he will always be remembered as a great player."

On the morning of the funeral Geordie's hearse arrived at the family home – where all the curtains remained drawn – a tradition in the North East and, to the families surprise, either side of the coffin stunning floral arrangements had been placed with red and while flowers spelling out the words 'Geordie' and 'Arsenal.' The family choice was for an arrangement of lilies to spread on the lid of the coffin, but they were overwhelmed at this wonderful, considered gesture from the club.

The family followed Geordie in the second car, which also included his close friend, Jack Anderson – who you will come to know – as well as brothers Joe and Norman. One of the older brothers, Eddie, met the family at the church and, along with Tom, Joe and Jack, would be a pall bearer. Tom acknowledges that helping carry his own father was tough but, as he said to his sister and mother at the time, it was the last thing he would be able to do for his father, so it was an important he did so.

The funeral directors were meticulous in every detail and had even thought to ask the police to cordon off part of Hills Road, where the English Martyrs

Roman Catholic Church is situated, because it was such a busy route and in preparation of the arrival of the three coaches from Arsenal. Unfortunately, the convoy from North London was held up in traffic, making them nine minutes late, which held up the service. I'm sure you can imagine the surprise among unsuspecting shoppers and workers when Arsene Wenger hurriedly lead Tony Adams, Patrick Vieira et al down the road towards the church.

Meanwhile, Tim, Jill's fiancée and Marj's nephews and nieces were handing out the Order of Service, on the front of which was adorned an image of a passionate, determined looking Geordie, which the family felt encapsulated the man. Many Arsenal fans turned up at the church too, asking if they could come in to send off 'one of their own' – the family knew Geordie would have been delighted – and it was important to them that nobody was turned away on the day. Monsignor Tony Rogers, who conducted the service, says that he has never seen the place so full before or since – over 500 people were crammed into the church – underlining the popularity of the man. Once the Arsenal contingent were seated, the four pall bearers carried the coffin into the church, followed by Geordie's brother Norman, then Marj and Jill.

The next wonderful surprise for the family was to be greeted at the door by two members of the old Metropolitan Police Band who had performed at half-time during almost every home fixture that Geordie had played in at Highbury – the two veterans, in full uniform, gave a white-gloved salute either side of the church entrance – it was hard to think of a more fitting tribute, or a gesture more appropriate, from the era in which he had graced. Geordie had great respect for the traditions and standards of Arsenal Football Club and would have approved, that much was certain.

The family recall being taken aback when, as they entered, the whole congregation turned as one to face them, they realised just how many mourners there were. At most funerals the mourners face forward, but Father Tony had decided to break with tradition as, in the order of service, it clearly states 'stand and face the back,' – the sound of everyone turning in unison was audible.

Every generation of Arsenal was represented in that church; the elder statesmen; those that had coached Geordie (Don Howe and Steve Burtenshaw); the Directors; his team mates from the Sixties and Seventies; fellow members of the coaching staff; the first team squad in its entirety and, of course, the youth and reserve teams, who felt the loss of their mentor as profoundly as any, particularly those who had been with him on that fateful day and witnessed events first-hand.

Jill and Marj shared the first reading, having rehearsed together in front of the bedroom mirror the night before. Jill remembers as she read to the mirror in her mother's bedroom she kept seeing her dad's face starring back at her, and it was not the face she wanted to recall, but the one she had just seen. The reading was to be 'Funeral Blues' by WH Auden, and Jill was asked to begin the poem as Marj wanted to read the third verse so she could recite the following words for the love of her life:

He was my North, my South, my East and West,
My working week and my Sunday best,
My noon, my midnight, my talk, my song,
I thought that love would last forever, I was wrong.

They were conscious that although it was not an uplifting passage, the poignant message summed up how they felt at the time and had wanted to present their words early in the service, accompanied by Tom, who held both their hands to give moral support. Indeed, Jill recalls introducing the poem by saying; 'this is how we are feeling at the moment.' Somehow they got through it and, for Jill's part, she recalls focusing on Patrick Vieira and David Seaman, because of their height. The next reading was from Bob Wilson who had been befriended by Geordie as soon as he arrived at Arsenal in 1963. Jill recalls vividly how he touched the coffin and shared a moment as he went up to address the congregation. Wilson was visibly shaken and moved, but read beautifully, as one would expect for an accomplished television presenter:

Believers Who Have Died

Brothers and sisters, we do not want you to be uninformed about those who sleep in death, so that you do not grieve like the rest of mankind, who have no hope. For we believe that Jesus died and rose again and so we believe that God will bring with Jesus those who have fallen asleep in him. According to the Lord's word, we tell you that we who are still alive, who are left until the coming of the Lord, will certainly not precede those who have fallen asleep. For the Lord himself will come down from heaven, with a loud command, with the voice of the archangel and with the trumpet call of God, and the dead in Christ will rise first. After that, we who are still alive and are left will be caught up together with them in the clouds to meet the Lord in the air. And so we will be with the Lord forever. Therefore encourage one another with these words.

Thessalonians 4 Verses 13-18

Holy Communion was taken by many, including several of the Arsenal players, during which time a beautiful choir and soloist sang Ave Marie, which has been described as a stunning and deeply moving performance by many of those who have contributed to this book.

Word of Remembrance, as described in the Order of Service, fell to Geordie's captain and his close friend, Frank McLintock. The family had no doubt

that Frank was the man for the task, but for Frank himself, he describes it as; 'one of the hardest things I have ever had to do.' Jill recalls him starting with 'I knew a Geordie once' but he froze, stopped, then moved on to other stories, but she already knew what he'd attempted to say – it is a story that Frank had always told Jill and it is one he shares later in this book – but it was, in essence, that having met Geordie Armstrong, he instantly felt warmth to all Geordies. Frank was clearly choked, but he continued, breaking down on several occasions, but sharing some wonderful memories and life-lasting impressions of his close friend.

Few reading this book will be aware of Geordie's obsession with the National Lottery, and the lengths he went to trying to win it. He made it his responsibility to run all the syndicates at Arsenal and it was a running joke with his family and those at the club that he was forever looking for lucky signs, or indicators on numbers, for the draw. As Lee Dixon said to me 'Geordie always seemed to have three passions in his life: his work, his family and the lottery!'

McLintock had planned to talk about Geordie's obsession, then tell a joke along the lines of half-expecting his old friend to pop up from the coffin, point to the hymn numbers, then tell the congregation of mourners that they were a sign from God that he was going to win the lottery, but he was uncertain how it would be received so he left that part out, but Jill knows her dad would have enjoyed the joke!

After the conclusion of the service, the family and close friends proceeded to the local cemetery where Geordie was to be buried. Virtually the whole of the 1971 squad shared a moment together around the grave. The togetherness of that team will probably never be surpassed in the history of our club and, in case you feel I generalise without foundation, Tony Adams, the then skipper, came over and commented on how astonishing it was, that 29 years after the Double, the bond remained so strong. Some might have been astounded that all bar two of that Double winning squad, including Bob McNab, who had flown in from America, were there, but as Charlie George said to Adams at the time; "Yes Tony, but this was Geordie Armstrong..." No other explanation was required.

Amidst all their shock, the family had overlooked a suggested charity that Geordie might have wished to assist, and consequently, the floral contributions were simply overwhelming. They came from friends, from the locals in Great Abingdon, from colleagues, from each department at Highbury and from virtually every club through the entire English League and from Scotland too. In addition there were contributions from numerous supporters and the 1971 team had arranged a red and white garland which read 'Geordie on the Wing'.

Nobody can prepare an individual, or be quite sure how grief will affect or change a person, but for Jill, who has been my collaborator and inspiration for this book, after a month off work, said she returned feeling a completely different person.

Both Jill and her mother said the sense that they were outside their own bodies, watching themselves doing things, stayed with them for ages. For Jill, in particular, there was a profound feeling of not fitting in anymore – and a grief counsellor eventually explained it is not uncommon to feel your whole life had changed when you lose someone so suddenly. However, for the Armstrong's, their lives genuinely had – they had lived a life dominated and dictated by football.

That purpose, that existence which revolved around Arsenal Football Club for so long, had disappeared almost overnight and even simple things like watching television together in the family home, when Geordie's finger would constantly hover over the remote control looking to move the channel to football, had changed forever.

And now, fourteen years later, there is clearly still a massive void in the lives of the Armstrong family. Nothing can compensate that loss but, in some small way, we hope this book will help all those who knew, admired and loved George Armstrong – a wonderful man, husband, father, friend, teammate and football icon – somebody who was taken far too early.

BEFORE GEORGE BECAME GEORDIE

George Armstrong was born into a working class Catholic family, the youngest of nine children. He grew up in a three bedroom semi-detached house at 9 Kipling Avenue Hebburn, County Durham, a small industrial town, situated south of the River Tyne between Gateshead and South Shields, to parents Edward and Elizabeth. George had six older brothers: Arthur, John, Edward, Jimmy, Norman and Joe and two sisters: Agnes and Ellen.

George did much of his growing up with his brothers Norman and Joe – ten and five years his senior respectively – as by the time he was old enough to play outside, the rest of his siblings had all flown the nest. So small was the house that as soon as the children left school and got a trade, they were expected to leave home.

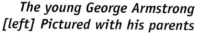

*The young George Armstrong
[left] Pictured with his parents*

August 9th 1944 was a day that Joe Armstrong, then aged five, remembers well... "It was a hot summer's day during the school holidays – I had been to Jarrow Park with the lads from our street, mostly pals my own age and one of two older friends of my brother Norman. After a day spent enjoying ourselves, getting into 'a right mucky state', we made our way home. On approaching our house, I was surprised to see a bicycle parked against our fence and, attached to the saddle, was a little black box. Norman and I immediately ran up the path and through the back door to investigate, only to be ushered away by our oldest sister, Agnes. The bike belonged to Nurse Adler, the local midwife, and she had just delivered the newest addition to the Armstrong clan – our little brother George."

George's was a simple, happy childhood in an era where everywhere, from streets, to parks, to coal mine slag heaps, were improvised playgrounds for local children. There was never a shortage of friends for George and his brothers to play with, games that were almost always played outdoors and predominantly sports related. Physical games were always at the top of George's agenda, and improvisation was usually required. The favourites were golf, with the links being the slag at Monkton Village pit, or cricket, played with a piece of wood from a neighbour's fence – or simply running races around the block.

In the summer the Armstrong lads would swim in the local lakes, take the bus to South Shields beach, or visit the fun fair. But whatever the activity George and his friends got up to, whether scrumping apples in late summer, snowball fighting in the winter, or even visiting the picture house in Jarrow, a football was never far from his feet.

Just up the road, at number three, lived George's close childhood friend, Kevin Connelly. Although two years George's senior, the two would walk to St Aloysius Roman Catholic school together and became good pals. St Aloysius appears to have a proud heritage when it comes to football. Former pupils include Johnny Dixon, who played over 400 matches for Aston Villa between 1945 and 1961, and Ray Wood, who starred for Manchester United and England – in fact Wood, later a Munich air crash survivor, married a girl by the name of Betty Lamb, who lived opposite the Armstrong's.

Kevin recalls how he and George became the envy of all the other kids in the street and at school when, during one close season, they had played football in the Lamb's back garden and had enjoyed taking shots against the England goalkeeper, who had just won the League title with United. Who would be the next great player to emerge from Hebburn I wonder?

Kevin also recounts George being competitive and enthusiastic about all sports as they grew up – in the days when few could afford a television, their live sport fix came via the radio. The duo would listen to Wimbledon, then rush out and mark up a court with chalk in the street. Then, in the summer of 1956, when the England selectors had recalled Cyril Washbrook at the aged 41 for an Ashes Test, they listened as the Lancastrian batsman hit a swashbuckling 98 to share a stand of 187 with Peter May to win the Second Test for England. Of course, creases and boundaries were soon drawn up in Kipling Avenue before the jubilant Test action was re-enacted.

Despite being strong academically, and a good sporting all-rounder, it was in football where George really excelled, and by the time he was 12, he was already playing in the school senior team, two years above his age group. Everyone was much taller than George, who was forced to play in an ill-fitting kit where the shirt hung down the leg of his shorts and had to be constantly hitched up. Connelly recalls how the opposition team's players would ask in disbelief, "Is he playing against us?" Most of the other lads were one to two feet taller than George, who was also short for his own age, let alone older boys. However, once the game had started, they would quickly realise why he was playing – nobody needed to ask a second time!

At that tender age of 12, such was his obvious prowess, George became the youngest player to represent Jarrow, Hebburn and Felling Boys, becoming something of a local celebrity owing to his exceptional ability. He was also selected by Durham County. His brother Joe recalls how, during his early senior school years, some foolishly mistook his younger brother's size for weakness, but that soon passed; "He took after our dad in height and stature – small and stocky – but had plenty of heart and guts. The old saying 'you can't beat a good little one' proved true throughout his life – both on and off the pitch."

George left school at 15 and found employment with the big local Ship-builders, Hawthorn Leslie, and at 16, started an apprenticeship as an electri-

[Front row, second from right]
George with the 1954/55 junior school team

cian – a path that two older brothers had already trodden – the three Armstrong lads becoming well known, and all played for the companies teams. Although Joe, a plumber, and George, an electrician, played together for Hawthorn Leslie in the local league, they also played against each other in the company's inter-occupational competitions. Joe was a useful player too, a tough-tackling defender who, in 1958, had signed a part-time contract for Leeds United. He admits that as a 21-year-old he struggled to catch and tackle his younger, speedier sibling. At the company sports day in the summer of 1960 Joe and George Armstrong entered virtually every track and field event and, between them, wiped the board. In fact it seems quite likely that George's legendary stamina and fitness can, without a doubt, be attributed to the two brother's competitiveness, and by George aspiring to be like Joe.

Joe was a keep fit fanatic and used to organise year-round training for any colleague, friend, or brother, who cared to join him. The sessions would consist of distance and sprinting runs, stamina building and occasional ball work. He would push the lads extremely hard and some would fall away, but never George, who thrived on it. The tougher the session, the more George enjoyed them, even on cold, wet nights they would train under the dim light emitted from the lamp posts which surrounded the ground.

Organised by Jimmy Hedley, who went on to become recognised as one of the UK's foremost coaches, with Steve Cram his finest pupil, the two brothers would usually also attend the Jarrow Athletics Club two evenings a week at a local school gym. As you read on, this book will underline what a phenomenal athlete Armstrong was on a football pitch for Arsenal Football Club, but it is already emerging what great preparation was being undertaken.

Whilst in his first full year at Hawthorn Leslie, in late 1960, George was invited to travel to Lincolnshire for a trial with Grimsby Town. As George was later to tell *Scorcher and Score* comic; "Due to a mix up I only played in the second half and that was on the right wing – a position I had never played before!" He described the whole experience as a disaster but, on returning to Hebburn, and before even hearing of Grimsby's rejection, he was to learn that Newcastle United wanted to have a look at him.

Armstrong went along and played a match for Newcastle's Juniors and impressed enough to be selected again – as a result he was asked to sign for the Tyneside giants as an amateur.

But what happened next, a simple misunderstanding, was to shape George's future. He was happily combining playing for the Hawthorne Leslie Electrician's team and for Newcastle Juniors, when one week's fixture clashed. "Our Shipyard side were in an important Cup Semi Final and were anxious that I should play for them, whilst Newcastle Juniors had also selected me to play the same afternoon. I chose to play for the shipyard – they'd treated me well and I was only an amateur at Newcastle. I made arrangements for Newcastle to be told that I would not be available to play for them. However Newcastle claimed that the message never got through, which created some friction between the club and myself."

According to brother Joe, whoever was in charge of Newcastle youth at that time clearly resented the situation and took it out on George. The Magpies continued to ask George to travel in for training, but refused to select him for matches – whether or not the petty coach wanted to teach young George Armstrong a lesson is unknown – but they must have eventually regretted their short-sighted outlook for years to come because young George, disillusioned with the situation, asked to be released from his amateur contract. When faced with this ultimatum United were reluctant to oblige, but George stood firm and, on the 31st January 1961, he got his wish.

A few months later a North East scout from a certain North London club spotted him and asked if he would like to come to London for a trial. Initially he was reluctant, soured by his experiences and treatment by the two professional clubs he'd had dealings with. However Joe convinced him to go – George taking time off work to travel down to Arsenal and take

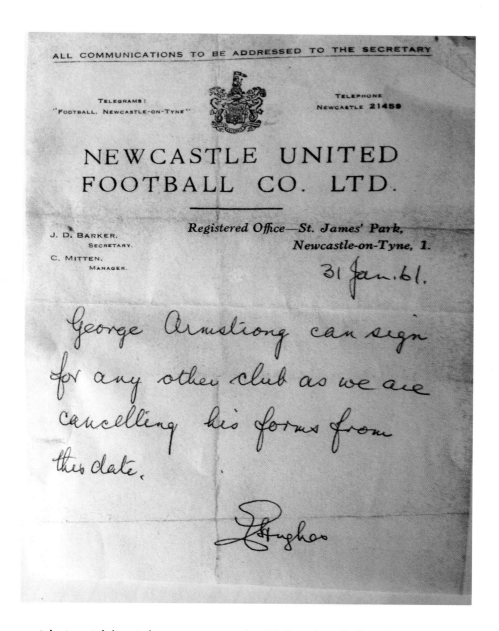

TELEGRAMS:
"FOOTBALL, NEWCASTLE-ON-TYNE"

TELEPHONE
NEWCASTLE 21459

NEWCASTLE UNITED
FOOTBALL CO. LTD.

J. D. BARKER,
SECRETARY.

C. MITTEN,
MANAGER.

Registered Office—St. James' Park,
Newcastle-on-Tyne, 1.

31 Jan. 61.

George Armstrong can sign for any other club as we are cancelling his forms from this date.

Hughes

part in two trial matches on consecutive Wednesdays (9th and 16th) during August 1961 and to follow his dream. Because Arsenal had invited several other inside-forwards along to the trial, George was again asked to play on the wing instead – it turned out to be a very fortuitous situation and those two days' holiday were ultimately time well invested because on the evidence witnessed during the two trials, the Arsenal manager, George Swindin, had obviously seen all that he needed before making his decision. On August 17 Swindin wrote the following letter to George.

Captain of the 1959 Jarrow, Hebburn and Felling Boys team

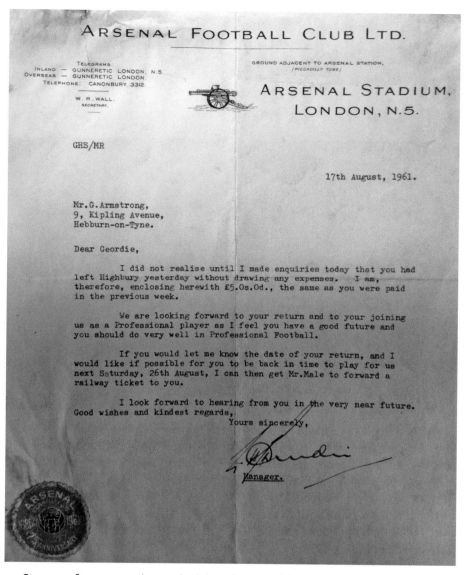

ARSENAL FOOTBALL CLUB LTD.

TELEGRAMS
INLAND — GUNNERETIC LONDON, N.5.
OVERSEAS — GUNNERETIC LONDON
TELEPHONE: CANONBURY 3312.

W. R. WALL,
SECRETARY.

GROUND ADJACENT TO ARSENAL STATION,
(PICCADILLY TUBE)

ARSENAL STADIUM,
LONDON, N.5.

GHS/MR

17th August, 1961.

Mr. G. Armstrong,
9, Kipling Avenue,
Hebburn-on-Tyne.

Dear Geordie,

    I did not realise until I made enquiries today that you had
left Highbury yesterday without drawing any expenses. I am,
therefore, enclosing herewith £5.0s.0d., the same as you were paid
in the previous week.

    We are looking forward to your return and to your joining
us as a Professional player as I feel you have a good future and
you should do very well in Professional Football.

    If you would let me know the date of your return, and I
would like if possible for you to be back in time to play for us
next Saturday, 26th August, I can then get Mr. Male to forward a
railway ticket to you.

    I look forward to hearing from you in the very near future.
Good wishes and kindest regards,

Yours sincerely,

Manager.

It was of course a huge decision for a lad just turned 17 to leave the
family in Hebburn and travel alone to live in the capital to pursue a career as
a professional footballer, but it was the right one, which made his family and
friends very proud. George would undoubtedly miss his family and friends but
his courage and determination to succeed once again shone through.

He was no doubt pinching himself daily in the final months of 1961 – but
the truth is he could continue to pinch himself for the next 17 years – George
Armstrong the electrician metamorphosed into Geordie Armstrong the Arsenal footballer then, ultimately, into 'Geordie Armstrong on the Wing'... an
Arsenal Legend.

WELCOME TO HIGHBURY

Seventeen-year-old George Armstrong arrived in London as a wide-eyed teenager, in a strange city, scarcely believing he was not still an apprentice electrician having to clock in at Hawthorn Leslie every morning. Ex-Gunner George Male was in charge of housing the young professionals and apprentices when they arrived at the club at the time, a responsibility that Arsenal, who were signing players from all over the United Kingdom and Ireland, took very seriously. For George Armstrong, Male chose well, housing the youngster with the then Arsenal first-team captain, Vic Groves. Armstrong later described Groves as a mentor and a man who had a huge influence on his career. Groves, along with his wife, undoubtedly took the young Geordie under their wing and, in many ways, Vic replaced Norman and Joe as the big brother figures in his life.

In 1961, when Armstrong arrived at Highbury, Arsenal were not riding high – the previous campaign had been unremarkable to say the least – with the club finishing 11th in Division One. So, how was a small, 17-year-old trainee sparkie from Hebburn likely to have any influence on the sleeping giant that Arsenal had become? Of course there is no substitute for first-hand knowledge, so I tracked down some of the men who played with Geordie in the early 1960s.

George Armstrong was not the only winger to arrive at Highbury in the summer of 1961 and, there is little doubt, that Geordie's arrival did not command the same newspaper coverage that was allocated to Johnny Macleod, the new sensation of Scottish football. Recently capped, and a record signing for a winger at £40,000, the 22-year-old from Hibernian, it would be fair to say, was the man manager George Swinden was pinning his hopes on to turn his side's fortunes – not Geordie.

Macleod recalls the first time he was introduced to Armstrong, with the suggestion that he was from 'his part of the world' by somebody whose strange geographical sense had bracketing a Scot with a Geordie! Macleod found this particularly ironic as, apparently, the Scots called Geordies 'Blackfaces' – a nickname derived from the coal mining heritage of the North East – the greater irony being that Armstrong was very pale-faced. Macleod's first impressions were of a player he describes as; "A mild mannered, polite, young lad, who found himself surrounded by grown men who were all so unlike him."

Johnny also recalls that the club put Geordie on a special diet to beef him up; "They recognised his talent, but were worried by his size. There was also some talk of sending him back home for a while, but such was his determination and hard work, that was never likely to happen." Geordie was clearly going to do whatever it took to succeed, that was evident early on, and he was fortunate to be lodging with Vic Groves and his wife, who overlooked the diet that would have been suggested by the club. Macleod remembers getting on well with Geordie, but despite once inviting him for dinner, they did not socialise much, due to the six-year age gap... "Geordie was not a big drinker, just an incredible trainer."

Ironically, Armstrong's debut in early 1962 [pictured left] came about when he was called in to replace an injured Macleod on the right wing. At the time the two first choice wingers were Macleod and Alan Skirton, both very direct, attacking wingers, with an eye for goal. This, however, was the problem for the team, which by that stage, was managed by Billy Wright. The Gunners were free scoring alright... they were also free conceding. The former Wolves ace had to find a way to change the balance of the team and the solution, as Macleod confirms, was Geordie Armstrong. "Geordie was doing what Alan and I weren't, tucking in when the team were defending. In those days the conventional winger just attacked when he got the ball." Macleod and Skirton were conventional wingers, as was the norm in the early 1960s, but Geordie offered a whole new option, which subsequently allowed the manager to change the emphasis and shape of the team in 1962/3, occasionally playing just one of the two attacking wingers, who could play on either flank, with the addition of Geordie for a more defensive shape.

By 1963/64 this was a permanent system and, on September 25, 1963, Macleod and Armstrong were the two wingers selected for Arsenal's first-ever game in European club competition – Macleod scoring the club's first European goal against Stævnet of Copenhagen in the Inter Cities Fairs Cup. At the beginning of the following season Macleod, after being voted player of the pre-season tour of South Africa, was sold to Aston Villa.

ALAN SKIRTON – ARSENAL 1959-1966

Alan Skirton had been unearthed by Arsenal from non-league Bath in 1959, the winger choosing Arsenal over Chelsea – a decision he's never regretted. However, soon after signing, he contracted tuberculosis but, despite the chronic illness, Arsenal stuck by him, with Bertie Mee, who was the team's physio at that stage, nursing him back to full health and fitness. In Geordie's first season Skirton hit an impressive 19 goals in 38 appearances from the wing and was undoubtedly one of the few success stories in the team during 1961/62 and, as such, his evaluation of his new team-mate, and as a competitor for his own place in the team, is a valued one. In a broad Bristolian twang Skirton is quick to underline the respect he had for Geordie; "The first thing I've got to tell you is that he was just a marvellous winger for Arsenal! He was quiet and football always came first. He also had stamina like no other player at the club. Together we gave Billy Wright the balance he wanted in the team." Skirton, a direct, fast winger, with a goal threat on one flank, Geordie, the hard working winger, with the ability to make goals for others, on the other. Both could play on either wing, so they often swapped during the game or at half time, and Skirton recalled a prime example, which came in an away match against Blackpool.

"I was on the left and Geordie was on the right... the right-back that day was the best in the League and at the time, England's first-choice, Jimmy Armfield. My game was all about speed, but I was getting nowhere against Jimmy. But after we swapped, Geordie gave him a torrid time!" He also joked that; "He ran his socks off in every match he played for the Arsenal, which was very unusual for a winger!"

Perhaps Skirton is too modest when he suggests that he was a winger who could only take defenders on with speed – whereas Geordie had more skill and subtlety to offer whenever pure pace was not working. Skirton scored 54 goals for Arsenal in 154 games which, for a winger, is a phenomenal return in the top flight, one which should not be overlooked.

Alan was eventually sold to Blackpool at the beginning of the 1966/67 campaign but is in no doubt that Armstrong should be remembered as one of the all-time Arsenal greats – a player who changed the whole complexion of side in the 1960s as well as bringing a new dynamic to wing-play. Skirton feels the legacy his former teammate has created has resonated through all successful Arsenal sides ever since.

So, with Billy Wright changing the shape of the team to employ one orthodox winger, plus Geordie, who were the fortunate Arsenal full-backs that had their load significantly lightened by Arsenal's unique box-to-boxer?

BILLY MCCULLOUGH – ARSENAL 1958-1966

Whilst Armstrong was completely at home on either flank, or with either foot, he was chiefly deployed on the left and Northern Ireland International, Billy McCullough, was the man lucky enough to consistently play behind Geordie for the best part of four seasons between 1962 and 1966.

To this day, McCullough remains in awe of the work-rate and talent his friend possessed; "There are simply not enough superlatives to describe the amount of ground Geordie covered for the Arsenal, over every blade of grass in every game back then. In my view, some of today's players aren't fit to lace his boots." It is also worth bearing in mind that McCullough was used to playing behind another George for his country in the mid-Sixties, one with the surname 'Best', so he certainly knows a good player when he sees one.

"Geordie could have been a left-back himself as he did so much work covering at the back and tackling. He was simply like no other player I'd played with – he was a breath of fresh air. I never had to worry about the opposition's winger because George had usually dealt with him first – I just picked up the scraps."

As we have heard, it was this ability to offer a totally different style of wing-play that caused Billy Wright to re-think the Arsenal set-up, however, as McCullough stresses, it was not just him who was grateful for the energy and ability of Geordie – the Arsenal strikers were also benefitting at the opposite end of the pitch.

Sadly, I cannot ask Joe Baker, a player who scored 51 League goals for Arsenal in two seasons between 1963-65, but if I could, McCullough is confident that a certain "Wee Geordie", as he will always be known to the Northern Irishman, would still be at the top of Baker's Christmas card list.

McCullough fondly recalls the relationship Geordie struck up in 1961 with another new arrival from County Durham, a centre-back by the name of Laurie Brown. "From the very first training sessions Brown felt the strength of George's tackle and christened his fellow county man 'You wee bugger'." He also names many other tough defenders who mistakenly thought they could bully the 'wee bugger' in the early days but, just like the lads two years his senior and two feet taller back at his school, they quickly realised the error of their ways.

DAVID COURT – ARSENAL 1962-70 & 1996-2014

It is fitting, that whilst we conclude the chapter that covers Geordie's early impact at Arsenal, I had the chance to speak with David Court, a player who not only worked with Geordie throughout the Sixties, but again in later years under Arsene Wenger. Few men knew Geordie better than David, who is one of the 'band of brothers' to join Vic Akers, Terry Murphy and Liam Brady (plus the Armstrong family) on October 31 each year to remember their friend.

Court, like Geordie, was born in 1944, but joined the Arsenal in a more conventional way in the July of 1959 – as a 15-year-old apprentice. As such, he is another perfectly positioned to assess the early impact of Armstrong when he arrived in the summer of 1961, and recalls the first time that he saw Geordie properly was in a Reserves v First Team match at Colney. "Geordie was up against the Arsenal and Northern Ireland right-back, Jimmy Magill, who was a quality defender known for his jockeying style..." Magill was 22 and at the peak of his powers but, in Court's own words; "Geordie murdered him!"

He also confirms that, in the early years, Vic Groves took Geordie under his wing and looked out for him both on the pitch and off it. Court describes his friend as; "The most generous person I have met – both of spirit and financially." He imagines there were some who would take advantage of his giving nature but not, at least in the early years, while Groves was keeping an eye out for him.

One of the most amusing early incidents Court recalls occurred when the then Board member, Reverend NF Bone, visited the training pitches, he

Arsenal's permanent fixture

explains; "Bone liked to take an interest in the new, young players, particular if they might be missing home and he'd asked to be introduced to Armstrong. Bone, who was slightly hard of hearing, then asked, "So young George, where have you come from?" To which Geordie politely replied, "Sir, I come from Hebburn..." This caused some consternation for the Reverend but the players found it hilarious!"

He also describes Geordie as; "Immensely powerful and dynamic..." and, like so many, reiterates that Geordie was the fittest player you were likely to see. "It was a standing joke at Billy McCullough's expense that Geordie was doing all his work and it was Geordie who kept him in the side. Billy thought it was as funny as everyone else and continually patted Geordie on the back and thanked him after each game. In all seriousness though, he truly was able to turn defence into attack for Arsenal, all on his own. Winning possession back in his own penalty box then instantly being on the run with the ball at feet all the way down the wing."

One of the key words that epitomised Geordie in his early career at Arsenal was 'determination', and Court insists there was a fire burning to succeed as a professional footballer within him, but; "It was success on the pitch and the respect of his peers that drove Geordie, not the fame and trappings off it. That was his nature and always stayed with him." Court offers an example away from the football pitch to sum up that never-give-up spirit perfectly.

"At the end of 1966/67 the squad were away on and end of season tour to Cyprus. Not many of the lads had water-skied before, but several decided to try it, me and Geordie included. As anyone who has attempted it will know, it is very difficult for a beginner, and the instructor tells you that if you fall, you should let go of the baton. Player after player tried, but few could get themselves upright, and if they did, for no more than a seconds or two. Then it was Geordie's turn. We all watched from the boat as he managed to pull his stocky frame upright and gain his balance before falling. He had done well, but this being Geordie Armstrong, full of determination and refusing to let it beat him, we all watch in amazement as he allowed himself to be dragged along, for what seemed like ages, in the water. Holding on for dear life with one hand, and trying to get the other back on the stick, all we could see of Geordie was an arm and a hand as he was dragged submerged through the waves – we didn't know whether to laugh or panic – but nobody was surprised that he refused to admit defeat and let go!"

When asked about Geordie being overlooked by England, Court has another tale to tell. Geordie once told him that after an Under-23 game for England, in which Armstrong had scored, he'd received a phone call from Alf Ramsey in which, according to Geordie, the national team manger had told him, in no uncertain terms, how well he had played, how impressed he was and how he saw a bright future for him. But, despite that vote of confidence, Armstrong was never to receive another call from Ramsey. It became a running joke among all the Arsenal players that; "If your phone rang and you were told it was Alf Ramsey, you should say you were not at home in case you suffered the same fate!"

As we've learned, Court and Armstrong were close friends, but he is very honest about his ability when he says; "Perhaps he was not the most skilful winger in the game at that time, but he was easily the hardest working and the best crosser of the ball. You would have to go a long way in football to find anyone you could describe as more of a team player than Geordie... He was just totally selfless and such a giving player – one that had the same generous spirit on the pitch as he always showed off of it."

To this day, Court genuinely does not know which foot Geordie actually favoured – he seemed equally comfortable and deadly-accurate with either. It was this ability, combined with his phenomenal fitness and work-rate, that allowed Billy Wright, followed by Bertie Mee, to design their teams around him. For Court, all great teams, and certainly those he has witnessed at Arsenal, have had the balance created by one genuine grafter, who allows the team to include one creative 'luxury' player.

With Billy Wright, it was mixing Geordie with Skirton or Macleod – but the real success came in 1971. Although Court had just left the club, he had already seen the options that Geordie allowed Bertie Mee in relieving George Graham of his defensive duties.

Court concludes that when Geordie was on his staff in 1997/98, even Arsene Wenger used the Wright/Mee formula – with Ray Parlour providing the box-to-box work-rate and cover, whilst Marc Overmars was given the freedom to rampage on the opposite flank.

When Bertie Mee took over from Bill Wright in 1966/67, his gradual rebuild began with most of the older players being moved on, and by the time David Court left in 1970, only Geordie Armstrong remained from the Swinden era. Amazingly, Geordie was to outlast most of the players form the early Mee era too.

Before we move on to the early success of Bertie Mee's tenure as Arsenal manager, I would like to wrap this chapter up with a written contribution from the late, great Dave Sexton – a man acknowledged as one of the greatest ever football coaches – the man who Bertie Mee had chosen to become his first-team coach.

"I first worked with George in the World Cup year, 1966. Bertie Mee had asked me to coach at Arsenal, which I was thrilled to do as I was born in Islington. I started work at Arsenal in the August, and after working with George for a while, I could not work out why he was not selected for England. He had everything. Skill, speed, was two-footed, had incredible stamina, had a good shot and could head the ball well. But, above all, he was a tremendous team player. I believe that, had he been given the chance, George would have had a Word Cup Winners' medal for sure."

IN CONVERSATION WITH THOSE WHO WON WITH HIM

In truth, recalling the impact and influence of a player on a team and on a club, without being able to analyse and scrutinise the plethora of statistics we all use today, could be difficult. Particularly so when that player is Geordie Armstrong and the providing of assists was his raison d'être in the team – an Arsenal team, that under the new leadership of Bertie Mee, was beginning to challenge in the late 1960s, then went on to win in the early 1970s.

But why would you need cold statistics and record books when you can talk to those who truly knew what Geordie Armstrong meant, not just to them, but to 'The Arsenal'? As mentioned in the preface to this book, it was only fitting that I should speak to the fans who adored him, but first and foremost, we should draw upon the knowledge of those who had first-hand experience of the man, the friend and the team-mate.

Frank McLintock was Geordie's captain and his friend and, as we have heard, the family saw it fitting that it should be Frank who shared recollections at the funeral. The duo were team mates for nine years at Arsenal, neighbours in North London and, later, Geordie was to be McLintock's first signing as a manager when he took over at the helm of Leicester City. They would often travel in to training together and he would consider Geordie a dear pal.

"Geordie was the most kind and considerate man you would ever have the privilege to meet..." is how Frank described him, but as somebody who; "had a naturally miserable face and loving to have a good moan. Indeed he was known for it among his team mates. He would often arrive at training in a poor temper, 'effing away at the world... It was his way!" But McLintock and everyone knew not to take that too seriously... "We all knew that as soon as they all laughed at him and 'took the Mick,' his face would break into a wide grin and be transformed."

"His generosity was legendary at Arsenal. Not just in buying extra rounds, even if he'd just bought one, but also with his time. Nothing was ever too much trouble for Geordie where his friends were concerned. If your car broke down, no matter where you were, it was Geordie you called and he would be there."

His skipper and friend claimed that in his 20-year playing career he never played with anyone fitter than George. "No one trained harder or had the same stamina. It was just like you wound him up and set him off – left-wing, left-half, left-back – he was everywhere on the pitch. At the same time he never failed to be back in position when the opposition was on the attack."

He suggests that it was a constant source of amusement to all that Geordie and Peter Simpson were so close. "Everything about them was the polar opposite. Geordie, the most gregarious, infectious character, with Simpson, the most laid back man you could ever meet. Geordie was the clean-living fitness fanatic, whilst Simpson was the chain smoker who seemed to inhale so hard you would have thought the nicotine reached his feet. George was always optimistic and believed the team would undoubtedly win, but Simpson was a worrier who usually grumbled that everyone was too quick for the Arsenal defence and would be found out. Of course when they crossed the white line, both were winners and gave their all for the Arsenal."

McLintock is one of many scholars of the game who cannot fathom how Armstrong was never selected to represent his county in a full international. No disrespect to Peter Storey from the same Arsenal team, who did win many caps under Ramsey, but Geordie was the one player who deserved it the most, surely? "No one at Arsenal in the late Sixties and early Seventies could understand Ramsey continually overlooking Geordie as goal supply-line." For

Frank, the explanation that Ramsey's 'Wingless Wonder' did not use conventional wingers is not good enough. "George could easily have tucked in and played the up and down midfield role and his work ethic was exactly what Ramsey admired."

Frank also confirmed, that as well as being the fittest of the Double winning era, Geordie was the fastest. McLintock once organised a race at Colney between Geordie and the newly arrived Peter Marinello in the spring of 1970. "Peter had arrived at Highbury with a grand reputation and was tagged the 'Scottish George Best.' He was a bit of a greyhound, but I felt Geordie would have the edge. The squad was split and money was changing hands each way, but ultimately, it was Geordie who won. It was tight, neck-and-neck over the first 85 yards of a course marked by corner flags, but George's strength told and he pulled away in the closing stages to win by five yards."

That, of course, was the same Peter Marinello that had been bought for a record fee in the January of 1970 – the first time Arsenal had ever spent six-figures on a footballer – and had arrived to 'replace' George Armstrong, or so it had been reported. Marinello managed that feat for about three months in the Spring of 1970 but, by April, Geordie was back in his rightful place... a place that he never really lost for another seven years. Frank suggested that he thought Marinello had been reputed to say, tongue in cheek, that his greatest contribution at Arsenal was to make George Armstrong a better player!

In December 1971 McLintock was interviewed by Norman Giller for the Daily Express series entitled 'Hidden Aces.' The feature asked First Division captains who they considered to be their team's hidden gems... The article revealed that he, and the whole team, unanimously nominated Geordie. It is a superb interview and one certainly worth quoting from as it succinctly encapsulates what Geordie meant to his captain and his team at that time.

"He's not just a footballer he's a marathon runner too! We've had George up our sleeves for years. Nobody has cottoned on to what a great asset he is to the team."

"George is the most unselfish, generous bloke I know. He hardly drinks but, if ever he is standing in company at the bar, he wants to buy all the rounds. This is the same 'give everything' attitude that comes through in his game. He runs and runs, and just when you think he is going to collapse, he starts running again."

"It's the same in training. Most of us are looking for an easy workout. Where's George? Running!"

"It's about time you newspaper boys woke up to George Armstrong. Apart from all the work he does he just happens to be the best crosser of the ball in the game. He can land the ball on a match-stick."

As we will discover later in the book, when I catch up with Norman Giller and few other newspaper boys, I don't think Frank needed to worry – they were all well aware of how good Geordie was both individually and for the

Arsenal team. In a final observation, McLintock confirmed that Geordie's influence and impression on him was so significant that, since knowing him, he will automatically take a shine to any Geordie he meets... until they prove him otherwise! That's some legacy Geordie!

PETER SIMPSON 1964-78

Playing alongside 'Big Frank' in that successful Arsenal team was Peter 'Stan' Simpson, and everyone I speak to tells me that Geordie and he were inseparable during that era.

Simpson was one of the last, true Double-winning legends to leave Arsenal, when he headed out to the States for a two-year stint in 1978, before turning his back on the game entirely. Unlike many of that team, he has not stayed in contact with the club and has little time for the modern players, or how television has changed the game – but he was delighted to discuss his old friend.

Simpson and Geordie were very close and this, at first glance, may have seemed incongruous, but from what I have learned about Armstrong, and in talking to Simpson, a shared modesty shines through. Simpson struggles with his memories of actual matches and incidents, but when it comes to Geordie, he was able to share a few gems.

The pair shared digs with four other young players when Geordie first arrived in 1961, so they got to know each other very well. Their personalities could not have been more different, as Frank McLintock explained, but they became firm friends regardless.

Simpson recalls that, in the Billy Wright era, the former Wolves idol had seemingly lost control of discipline and that some senior pros did not respect him and called the shots... "It was only when Bertie arrived that the squad begin to gel, which was assisted by away trips abroad and to Blackpool." Trips on which, as was the case for most away matches, he and Geordie roomed together. "Mee was very strict and keen to have a team of fit athletes, which he of course managed, but no one came close to Geordie."

Simpson recalls with amusement that on away trips they would be instructed to be off to their beds to get a good night's sleep by Howe and Mee ahead of the match the next day. "While he was getting into his PJs Geordie would be down to his vest and underpants doing repeated sit ups and press ups next to his bed."

He also recalls Geordie's heart of gold and his generosity. "He was, in truth, too generous and some people could have taken advantage of this. Of course none of his team mates did though – he was universally loved and respected by the whole group."

'Stan' affectionately describes how he knew when Geordie was fed up or feeling the strain as he would subconsciously have his 'bottom lip up.'

Peter knew that, for Geordie, every day he spent as a footballer at Arsenal was an honour and a privilege to him. Consequently, "He always strove to work harder and be better, while some others took their new-found status for granted." He was also, as a result, genuinely modest about his ability. "He loved Arsenal and everyone at Arsenal loved him, players, staff and fans alike."

Geordie's friendship for Peter meant that he was continuously trying to energise and gee-up his languid team-mate and, as Eddie Kelly told me, and Peter repeated, he was told; "Listen Geordie, you just concentrate on doing your job and I'll try my best to do mine."

As well as rooming together, the pair invariably sat together on coach or train and played cribbage and gin rummy, which were the card games of choice. They were usually joined by John Radford and another partner.

Peter used to get involved in charity work and he always roped a willing Geordie into visit schools for the deaf and blind or, on occasion, even play disabled basketball. "Geordie was always willing and pleased to give back in any way he could." These trips were arranged off their own backs rather than organised club visits.

Like so many, Simpson describes the incredible work Geordie put in on the pitch; "I used to get exhausted just watching him."

Simpson's favourite memory, which he saves until last, was from a match... "It was the perfect cross for Ray Kennedy to head home and secure the League at White Hart Lane." I have a feeling he will not be alone in mentioning that moment!

EDDIE KELLY - ARSENAL 1969-76

Another player to feature high in Arsenal folklore, as well as high up the list of Geordie admirers, is Eddie Kelly. A team mate of Geordie's for seven years, who shared the highs of the Fairs Cup, the League and the FA Cup, and somebody who scored in both finals. Kelly even took over from McLintock as Geordie's skipper – in fact only Tony Adams has captained the Gunners at a younger age.

Kelly was effusive in his praise of Geordie and his opening observation proved very interesting – namely it is Kelly's sure contention, that while many pundits say players from their era would not have been able to play in the modern day; "Geordie would, without question." Eddie believes that Geordie would fit right into an Arsene Wenger Arsenal side; "Quick, incredible engine, perfect close control and perfect with the left or right. He was the best crosser of the ball I've ever played with, or have ever seen."

"Geordie had phenomenal fitness and was always there to cover you... he never failed to support Bob McNab at left-back. And I'm convinced that is why George 'Stroller' Graham always wanted to play on the left of the central-midfield area, so Geordie could be his legs."

Eddie said that Geordie would get embarrassed by all the praise he got because he was so modest, but the reality was, praise was constant; "No-one ever had a bad word to say about him. Even the opposition couldn't hate him because, no matter how much he tormented their full-backs, he always did it with a smile and never retaliated or moaned when he got kicked." Eddie told me that Joe Kinnear, who was the right-back at Spurs back then, said Geordie was the hardest opponent he ever played against. I hope you will find it interesting to read the views of other right-backs of the era later in the book.

Even Peter Marinello, who had every reason to feel bitter towards Geordie, could not be. "Geordie's attitude when the Peter arrived was not one of resentment, it was more of a case of just rolling up his sleeves, accompanied by a 'nobody's going to take ma fuckin' place' attitude." Another problem was that Peter was an individualist with flair at a time the Arsenal side was build around eleven team players... "Geordie was the ultimate team player. He would also always be in the top three at everything, whether it was cross-country or sprints, it made no difference to Geordie."

Eddie remembered the second leg of the Inter City Fairs Cup at home to Anderlecht and said that; "Bertie Mee had the Highbury pitch heavily watered to give the British style game the advantage but, of course, it made it tough on the legs. It did not affect Geordie though, it was like every time you got the ball, wherever you were on the pitch, Geordie was there next to you waiting to receive a pass. He must have covered every blade of grass and was easily the man of the match. It was like we had twelve men on our team with Geordie that night."

His impression was that Geordie was destined to be a great coach but not, for him, a manager. "He simply was too nice, too honest and could not be two faced enough." Geordie's nature meant he was the ideal coach with huge knowledge of the game, but always encouraging, looking for the positives and there with an arm around the shoulder or a willing ear.

For Kelly, his friend was Arsenal through and through; "He would not allow anyone to say a bad word about the club."

Kelly left me in no doubt how he felt: "I just loved the wee man. I can't say enough about him. He would not say a bad word about anybody and I doubt you will find anybody to say a bad word about him."

BOB MCNAB – ARSENAL 1966-75

Kelly highlighted, as have all his team mates, how Geordie could be attacking one second, then back supporting his full-back the next, so perhaps it was time to hear from the lucky man himself.

McNab describes Geordie as; "Generous to a fault. He would do anything for anybody and he was just the same on the pitch, giving of himself for the team." Playing behind Geordie, McNab describes as; "An absolute pleasure.... He was always there when I needed him and I hope Geordie felt the same in return."

McNab believes that, as a footballer, he will always remember Geordie most for his ball-striking ability and reiterated that George Armstrong "Was the best two-footed ball-striker he has ever seen. The only two others to compare would be Alan Hinton (Derby Country) and Bobby Charlton."

McNab would just stand back and admire Geordie's corner kicking from both sides, which was something to behold... "Off a three-step run-up he could deliver the football, with perfect flight, power, trajectory, swerve and bend... whatever was required at the moment." McNab doubts there is a player who can do the same today.

"Geordie had a special ability to be sprinting to the goal-line and still deliver a perfect cross on the run – without slowing at all – from either side of the pitch. And, if the move broke down, in the blink of an eye, he would be back tackling an attacker on his own goal-line."

"Geordie always had energy to spare and, in training, while the rest of us would be gingerly warming ourselves up on a cold winter's morning at Colney, Geordie would come flying out of the dressing room, banging footballs like missiles all over the field, laughing and shouting 'Come on let's get going!'"

He concludes by underlining that, in the ten years he played with Geordie, and as a friend for more than 30, what strikes him the most is that Geordie was exactly the same off the field, as he was on it. "In all my years of knowing Geordie I cannot think of a time when I heard anybody say a bad word about him. Seeing him away from football you could never have imagined he was a great footballer – so unassuming, completely without an ego. That's so unusual in our business."

The Arsenal side in the late Sixties and the early Seventies owed much to the success of its left-flank and, in much the same way that Cole, Vieira and Pires worked so effectively in more recent years – the Double-winning team of 1971 had McNab, George Graham and Geordie Armstrong... Which brings us nicely to another of the Gunners' prodigal sons.

GEORGE GRAHAM – ARSENAL 1966-72

It is clear that George Graham is a man that played a significant part in Geordie's career and it was he who persuaded his old team mate to return to Arsenal's coaching staff in 1990... Not that it took much persuading I imagine. Much of Graham's input into this book are memories from this latter part of his career and his thinking when asking Armstrong to run his reserves – but he did share some thoughts on their time playing down the left hand side for Arsenal.

"Bob McNab was one of the finest, tackling defenders, but that was his strength. His job was to win the ball and feed it to me and I, in turn, would

Bob McNab with Geordie Armstrong

look to release Geordie down the wing." He explained that so many of Arsenal's goals in that era came that way. McNab to Graham, Graham to Armstrong and Armstrong crossed for Radford or Kennedy to head home.

Of course Geordie would run all day and in reality did Graham's share of defensive duties. Bertie Mee's side was built on team spirit, talent of course and hard work. Geordie epitomised that side and led by example and his infectious nature rubbed off on his colleagues. Graham observed that he tried to mould his own sides the same way and stressed that special talent alone was never enough for Arsenal or for him. "The great footballers are those who have talent, combined with professionalism and a willingness to work hard."

Dave Sexton, in his time at Chelsea, then later, at Arsenal, showed that he was one of England's greatest-ever coaches and Graham recalled that he used to believe in the Barcelona way; "That every player should be good enough and comfortable enough to play in any outfield position. Geordie was perhaps one of the few at Arsenal who could play anywhere barring positions where his height was a disadvantage. He could have played, and did play, on both wings, but equally, he could have played in the centre of midfield, as an inside-forward, or in either full-back position." I think every Arsenal fan reading this book will know exactly how much of a task-master George Graham was, so for praise such as this to come from him, is high praise indeed.

PAT RICE – ARSENAL 1966-80 & 1984-2012

Pat Rice is another individual to have given Arsenal Football Club outstanding service and phenomenal commitment over the past fifty years, and few are better qualified to offer their opinion on Armstrong.

Rice, who has faced a battle with cancer in recent months, was delighted to be invited to participate in this chapter and wasted no time in saying that; "Geordie was just a complete gentleman who would do anything for anybody."

"I should be able to say this about every player I played with or coached at Arsenal but, the truth is, I can't. But with Geordie you knew that every single game he played in the shirt you would get 90 minutes out of him."

I mentioned to Rice that I had interviewed several full-backs about how it was to play against him, to which he quipped; "I'm glad I never had to do it in a match – it was bad enough that I had to do it in training. The truth of the matter was that for most full-backs, once he had gone past them, that was it, they just could not catch him!"

Rice went on to say that; "The players occasionally called Geordie 'the tennis machine' because, in the same way you could pre-programme the machine to serve tennis balls where you wanted them, you could ask Geordie exactly where you wanted the ball crossed. This was used in training for heading and volleys because he was just so uncannily accurate. Then, in matches, Radford, Kennedy or Graham just had to point and make their runs for Geordie to know where to flight the cross."

Rice describes football, both as player and as a coach, as a tough profession in which you very much have to earn respect, but with Geordie, you only had to meet the man. "He had so much warmth and was just so funny... but come three o'clock on a Saturday, you knew you'd have a warrior next to you."

There were no defenders that frightened Geordie and, according to Rice; "If anything, the tougher the tackles, the better he seemed to play. It was almost as if he took them as a compliment."

PETER STOREY - ARSENAL 1962-77

Often the hard man responsible for breaking up the opposition's attacks back in 1971 was Peter Story, who is held in the highest esteem by Gunners of a certain age and exactly the kind of defensive midfielder they would love to see in the role today.

Storey, who had just joined as a 16-year-old apprentice, remembers the diminutive Armstrong arriving for his trial in the summer of '61 and, in his mind, there was no doubt that the Arsenal scouts had "unearthed a gem in Geordie."

It was not until October 1965, however, that Storey was to join Geordie in the first team, coming in for the injured left-back, Billy McCullough, then playing 20 consecutive games, 16 of which were positioned directly behind Armstrong and offering defensive support for a player he described as; "A winger with a difference!"

Storey, who got his own break in the England side in a 3-0 win over Greece at Wembley in 1971, before going on to play a further 18 games for his country, described his team mate "as extremely unlucky not to win a cap at the same time I did – he's probably one of the best players ever *not* to do so." He understood the theory about Ramsey not selecting wingers after 1966, but observed; "Geordie was so much more than a conventional winger and, being completely two-footed could easily have played left or right-midfield in the Ball or Peters role."

Of course Arsenal did buy a high profile, more traditional, winger in Peter Marinello who, for a time, took Geordie's place in the team, but Storey's comment regarding his threat to Armstrong's long-term place was short, and to the point... "All the players knew Geordie would be back in the team."

"Geordie gave opposition full-backs a torrid time down either wing – he created so many of Arsenal's goal scoring opportunities, and with headers of the ball of the quality of Radford, Kennedy and Graham, a fair few were taken."

The whole Double-winning side worked hard and were extremely fit but; "Geordie was probably the fittest and probably worked the hardest... and the Arsenal crowd loved him for it."

BOB WILSON - ARSENAL 1963-74

Wilson described his friend Geordie Armstrong to me thus; "Geordie was our Ozil, except he worked much harder!" He went on to add "He was a box-to-box player and there were none of them in 1971!"

Wilson wanted to start at the beginning, when he arrived at Arsenal in 1963 wearing a duffle coat and a college scarf. "Everyone else made it clear that they assumed I couldn't make the grade because I was an amateur. It was only Geordie and Don Howe that treated me with respect and accepted me for who I was." Wilson had recently finished his degree and had to then do a year of teaching in London to be a qualified teacher. "I had been invited to train as an amateur with Arsenal and arrived looking every bit the middle class student... you can imagine the look on their faces! 'Who is this idiot?"

Wilson taught during day at Rutherford School and trained on Monday and Thursday nights. Then, when he finished the year and had qualified, was offered full-time professional papers in summer of 1964. "In that first year you have to pass the test with the rest of the boys. 'Can you play or can't you play?' And because Bob had been an amateur, most thought he would not be good enough to follow Jack Kelsey.

Even when Bob got in the squad and had played eight games, including one European match, a sequence that saw just one defeat, he found himself dropped after some of the senior players had spoken with Billy Wright. However, all through this difficult rite of passage, Wilson found Little Geordie, with his strong accent, was always kind and supportive – regardless of what the senior pros felt. Wilson would never forget this kindness and a lifelong friendship was formed.

Wilson agreed that no one had a bad word to say about Geordie, which is credit to him, as he was never afraid to speak his mind. "If he thought you were poor, or not pulling your weight, he would tell you, but always in such a way that you accepted it and he would never do it in front of the group. It was largely because he hated losing so much..." reflects Wilson. "However, it was so rare that anyone had cause to criticise Geordie. When we lost the ball he became a defender, if we had the ball, he was an attacker, his range spanned all 120 yards of a football pitch."

Wilson describes the outstanding energy and searched for the right words, before settling on just two... "Perpetual motion! Where the hell did he get the energy from? The thing you have to remember was that it was not the modern day, with perfect pitches and a light ball, we wore heavy boots, played on churned up bloody pitches with a heavy ball, which obviously he

had to cross at the end of it!" According to Wilson, the measure of Geordie's greatness was defined by how he delivered under pressure in the two defining games for his club and his team.

"If you look at the Fairs Cup in the First Leg we were three-nil down with a few minutes to go and looking down and out. The ball to Kennedy, which got us back in the tie, was from Geordie."

Then, in the Second Leg, Geordie provided the ball for Eddie Kelly to start the comeback at Highbury, Wilson feeling that night was the defining moment for that team and Geordie was the best player on the pitch. "That night against Anderlecht was the greatest match of Geordie's career and I know many supporters would agree."

"Then, of course, there was the night at White Hart Lane when we won the League. The pressure was enormous. Arsenal had to draw nil-nil or win, anything else and Leeds were Champions. Pat Jennings pushed a ball out in the 88th minute – Geordie kept it in play – then crossed it so perfectly for Kennedy to score the winning goal."

Wilson felt it was unfortunate that Geordie's greatest moments where never at Wembley; "But when you were like Geordie, everyone expected a certain performance level, and 99% of the times, that's what you got."

Wilson says that back in 1963 the players were only on about £30 a week and by 1971, perhaps £100 a week, but no matter what they earned, one thing's for sure; "The boys were drinkers. Any time we were on tour or allowed to have a drink, anything between seven and 15 pints was not unusual. But anywhere, any time, there'd be a group at the bar and there were drinks – Geordie would be knocking people out of the way to get to the bar." Wilson admits he would happily sit back and wait his turn, or not take one as he was not a drinker... "But neither was Geordie and he always insisted on buying the first round!"

He also remembers that all the squad were driving Ford Cortinas, or similar... "Then one day at training Geordie pulled up in a Jag!" Wilson recalls everyone joking and asking if he could see over the steering wheel! "Or is he sitting on cushions?!?" Bob said he admired that. Geordie obviously thought; "Bugger what the lads think, I am going to live my life!"

Geordie and Wilson always had a relationship of mutual trust and felt able to share problems and gripes with each other. In fact, on the morning of the day Geordie died at Colney, Geordie had been complaining in the canteen to Wilson over a cup of tea that he was undervalued and under paid by the club – he was thinking of having a word. Wilson adds; "Geordie had a point, the plain truth was that he was worth more."

After their brief discussion at Colney on that fateful day, Wilson left to go home and change, before heading on to the ITV studios to prepare for a Champions League show. During the afternoon a message had been sent to Bob informing him that Geordie had collapsed with a brain haemorrhage, then, during the evening, came the update he'd dreaded – that Geordie had passed away. Wilson, whilst extremely distressed, still had to present the show. "I was watching the wires as the news was confirmed, then had to write a tribute and read it out on air. I didn't manage to get through it without choking." It was one of the hardest thing he'd had to do on air as they two had been close.

Bob tells the story of how virtually the whole of the 1971 team was at Geordie's funeral; "There was a huge hole in the ground and just the 70/71 team standing around staring at the coffin. Tony Adams came over and was incredibly moved – he said 'What you have here, we will never see again. Look at my team now, they will all be scattered around after we retire.' Adams was close to Geordie too, but he was just overwhelmed by the closeness of our old team mates." Wilson thinks someone, possibly Frank McLintock, had responded along the lines of; "Yes Tony, but this was Geordie Armstrong!"

For Bob Wilson it remains a great sadness that Geordie is no longer with us because, ironically; "he was the most alive of them all. Even on the day he died Geordie could still be seen tearing around the training ground passing on his wisdom and knowledge."

He also still cannot believe that Alf Ramsey and Don Revie overlooked Geordie – he even went as far as to call it an insult. "Geordie's performance for Arsenal were massive and I still finds it unbelievable to this day that he was never selected for England."

When Arsenal fans voted George Armstrong the 40th best player in our club's history we have to accept that the poll was internet based and 'commissioned' in the recent era. To have the likes of Kanu, Petit, Nicholas, Williams and Talbot ahead of Geordie is, quite frankly, risible – but what Arsenal.com did get spot on, was parts of the description:

"He (Geordie) was an inspired exponent of precision crossing - it was estimated that the wide-man had a hand in more than half of the goals scored in the Double season of 1971.

At the peak of his powers the theory was simple: if you don't stop Armstrong, you don't stop Arsenal. His tireless energy was one thing, but his scalpel-sharp precision from the byline made Armstrong the player he was. Messrs Radford and Kennedy had much to be thankful for."

It is probably time to catch up with one of those aforementioned men who 'had much to be thankful for'...

JOHN RADFORD - ARSENAL 1964-76

John Radford is another former team-mate who is quick to highlight Geordie's giving nature and proves, once more, that it is sometimes simple acts of kindness, as well as what we achieve in life, that judges us as human beings... "Geordie was probably the most generous person I ever met. His nature was always to be the person who would say 'I'll get this.' In those days we got trains to away matches and George would always be the one to buy the teas and coffees, sandwiches or meals. He just would not let others pay and he always insisted it was on him. Even though George was not a big drinker he would always be in the pub and buying the first round."

Being such a clear beneficiary of Armstrong's artistry, it was essential to ask Radford about Armstrong's legendary crossing ability, about which he explains; "We first played together in the Arsenal reserves in the Metropolitan League – the balls were still the old leather ones with the laces tied and then tucked in. George was such a good crosser that I used to joke with him and say 'George when you cross the ball make sure the laces are on the other side of my head!' George's reply was always the same... 'I'll see what I can do John!'"

He went on to elaborate; "Wherever Ray or I made our runs... near-post, penalty spot or far-post, George could put the cross within a square yard from either flank and with either foot." He could land a cross on the proverbial sixpence.

Sadly, there are no actual records that show 'assists' from 1971 and, as a consequence, there are no statistics showing exactly how many of the 47 goals Radford and Kennedy scored in the Double-winning season were set up by Geordie. But, according to the man at the top; "Geordie would have been directly or indirectly involved in most of them..." Armstrong's wing play was the key to their success.

When I asked him about Geordie never being capped by England – John accepted the theory of Sir Alf Ramsey not operating with conventional wingers, but he personally felt the England boss; "Did not have much time for the Arsenal."

"George would have fitted easily into the modern game where wide men are expecting to work back because George did so all the time... (laughs) all Bob McNab had to do was pick up the pieces after George had tracked back to win the ball!"

Another fond memory was from the away trips when; "George and Peter Simpson would always play cards. There was always three people, those two, plus whoever fancied it on the day, playing gin rummy for a penny a point."

Radford was certainly not surprised when Geordie evolved into a coach back at Arsenal; "He was always a student of the game and loved every aspect of it, so it was almost inevitable that he would want to stay in the football world he loved so much, and in his nature to want to give something back."

RAY KENNEDY – ARSENAL 1968-74

If I am honest, I had not thought I would be in a position to write this section – Ray Kennedy has been suffering the awful effects of Parkinson's disease for 30 years now. He was not able to be at his friend's funeral and, since the 1990s, has seldom left his home, where he copes and lives a quiet life. Karl Coppack, one of three Liverpool fans who helped organise the 'Ray of Hope Appeal' in 2008, assisted me in making contact with the great man. Kennedy, via his son, has thanked me for writing this long-overdue book about his mate and provided the following is his moving contribution.

"Geordie was fantastic towards me when I first joined the club. Being a fellow Geordie myself, he took me under his wing and looked after me when I first moved to Arsenal. He also used to drive me back up North too, which really helped me settle as, being so young, it was nice to have someone from the same area helping me out. He was a great man and also a tremendous crosser of the ball. His cross for my goal at White Hart Lane in 1971 was fantastic and, for that alone, he deserves his place as an Arsenal legend."

I have nothing more to add – I am just so delighted that Ray Kennedy is part of this tribute – it would have felt incomplete without him.

JON SAMMELS - ARSENAL 1963-71

In the Sixties, John Sammels knew Geordie as well as most – the pair lodging together at Mrs. Girling's in Enfield Road – and a time, Sammels tells me; "when young Geordie was courting Marj!" After retiring from football, then became a driving instructor, one of his most notable successes was in getting a young Jill Armstrong, my collaborator on this book, through her driving test.

Sammels describes Geordie as generous to a fault... "It was in his DNA, his character and nature as a person, and that translated onto the pitch. His personality made him the perfect footballer for the Arsenal style of the late Sixties and early Seventies. Bertie Mee and Don Howe's Arsenal was about the collective and not the individuals and Geordie always played for the team. It was never about personal glory or attention for Geordie, he just wanted to provide crosses at one end and then support Bob McNab at the other."

Sammels commented on his friend being constantly overlooked by Ramsey and England; "It was odd as there were few players in that era, so brilliantly two-footed and with such stamina. Ramsey was intensely loyal to those who had not let him down, meaning that Ball, Charlton and Peters effectively picked themselves." As to why George never even made the squads, Sammels had no answer, although just as John Radford had alluded, he suspected that; "Possibly the England manager just did not really like the Arsenal?"

It was time to ask about his memories of Armstrong on the glorious April evening in 1970 that silverware returned to Highbury, the Inter City Fairs Cup Second Leg against Anderlecht, when Arsenal, having trailed 3-1 from the away leg in Belgium, won 3-0 to secure the club's first trophy in years – of course it was Sammels himself who scored the clinching third goal, but his abiding memory was Geordie's performance. "On that, and so many other nights, I marvelled at Geordie's ability. He could go past people for fun."

Sammels affirmed that whenever the ball went wide, there was an overwhelming belief from Kennedy and Radford, that the cross would come; "Nobody ever doubted that George would deliver because he was simply the best winger in the League – a truly amazing winger."

On the subject of Geordie's legendary fitness levels, he remembers that in pre-season training at Arsenal, there would be a very hard session in the morning, a few hours break, then an equally strenuous session in the afternoon. "Everyone else had collapsed after a light lunch, resting and dreading the next session. But George would be walking around with a tennis racket trying to find someone to have a game with him before the afternoon's training!"

In his 15 years playing at the top level of the English game, notching around 535 games split fairly evenly between Arsenal and Leicester City, Sammels confirmed that he had never played with or against a better crosser of the ball than George Armstrong. "In my eyes the most accurate deliverers of a cross from that time were Geordie Armstrong and Alan Hinton – who won two titles in 1972 and 1975 with Derby County. Few came even close."

CHARLIE GEORGE – ARSENAL 1968-75

Charlie George's admiration for Geordie began before he even became a player – Charlie had grown up watching Arsenal from the North Bank and, as a young lad on the terraces, he recalls watching him break into the first team at just 17. Speaking as a fan, George remembers; "We loved him straight away... when he lost the ball he would chase and hardy for the team."

As a colleague, he recognises that the whole team had a wonderful, spirited attitude; "But it seemed that Geordie was just a touch more industrious, he was a winner who hated to lose. We all did, but he took it harder than most. Geordie was always the fittest player at the Arsenal... only Archie Gemmill could compete with Geordie on that front." And Armstrong's lust for life was equally strong according to Charlie; "Geordie was one of those people who probably felt there were not enough hours in the day. When he was asleep, he probably felt he was missing out!"

George understood full well exactly why Geordie wanted to be back at Arsenal even, though he described the Reserve team role as; "A God-forsaken one." Leaving a club like Arsenal is never easy, and if you get an opportunity to come back and work in any capacity, you jump at it; "I suppose when he left Arsenal Football Club he obviously realised, like the rest of us did, there is only one football club. Arsenal is different class – there is no other club run as well as this one."

He concludes by suggesting that Geordie Armstrong was the perfect example of an 'Arsenal Man' both as a player and as a coach; "All the young

Bertie Mee with his 'players' player'

players respected him and enjoyed working with him, as had his team mates. It seems that everyone that was lucky enough to know him, at any level, loved him."

Having wrapped up the previous chapter with the considered opinions of Dave Sexton, it is perhaps appropriate that we should end this one with the views of the two men who coached, and managed, Geordie, as well as guiding Arsenal to glory.

THE COACHES VIEW: DON HOWE ARSENAL 1967-71 & 1977-86

Don Howe helped coached Arsenal to European and domestic triumphs, before later returning to support Terry Neill – then managed Arsenal himself in the 1980s. Sadly, Howe is suffering from Alzheimer's, but he still wished to speak to me about "one of his boys". Don was keen to stress that the Arsenal team he coached, and Bertie Mee managed, grew into their success by working hard together. "We trained the players hard, but the training was also fun – that was the key. The Double-winning side was the fittest team I ever worked with, but Geordie was the most naturally fit player of the whole squad – with only Pat Rice running him close. Geordie never lagged at all in matches and constantly worked back. He'd also arrive back for pre-season in top condition and never ever seemed to have to work at it like some of his team mates."

Don agreed that the accuracy of Geordie's crossing was another key strength; "That was integral to the way that side played and it was con- tinuously worked on in training. Crossing in match-play situations formed a central part of our training."

Oddly, Don stressed that he didn't see George as an out-and-out winger and, as such, like so many, does not understand why George never got 'that' call up. All he would say on Sir Alf Ramsey's position was that; "Different managers and coaches see different things, and want different things, eve- ryone has their favourites." The implication perhaps being, as others have hinted, that Arsenal players, no matter how strong their candidacy, were up against it at that time with that manager at the helm.

THE MANAGER'S VIEW: BERTIE MEE 1966-76

I will not claim to have adopted Doris Stokes-like powers and having been able to speak with Mee, but I have at least succeeded in unearthing some telling words of his own that formed the tribute at Armstrong's testimonial, which has been reproduced with the club's kind permission.

"Geordie – this great club player – has many attributes, which have made every League manager admire him. He has proved his consistency, not just through ninety minutes of a game, but for season after season. He had a natural enthusiasm as a young player and now, after five hundred games, this same enthusiasm is still with him. His work-rate, not just for himself, but for his team, has made him a "Players' Player." His unselfishness, both on and off the field, has meant that Geordie has always put the club before his personal gain. Indeed, he has never once caused any problems for me, his manager, either on or off the field. He is a great example to all young players. In fact his enthusiasm, skill and running to help his colleagues is probably unparalleled in the game. If there were eleven George Armstrong's in any one team, that team would win a major honour every year! If I may summarise his qualities on a very personal note, I would like to say, with all sincerity, that it has been with a great feeling of pride that I have had him on my staff. I only hope that in some small way, I have helped him towards reaching his many great achievements, of which, he must be justifiably proud. We, at Arsenal, are very proud of him."

This is a beautiful, heart-felt tribute from the man who brought glory back to Arsenal, and it leaves us in little doubt that Mee felt Geordie Armstrong was integral to his team's success. He includes this phrase 'he is a great example to all young players,' as at that time, Mee's Double-winning side was breaking up, with new, young players pushing to be part of the new Arsenal. Perhaps these new stars would benefit from the knowledge and example of Geordie Armstrong?

VIEW FROM THE OPPOSITION

After hearing from so many wonderful players who starred along-side the great man, and from those who worked with Geordie on the training pitch, his colleagues, the people who knew him best, I thought it would be fascinating to find some broader views on his prowess. As wonderful as his teammates' memories are, away from the training pitch, the players we've heard from so far did not actually have to face Geordie on the pitch. Yes, they witnessed Armstrong first-hand terrorizing opposition full-backs, but what was it like to be one of those defenders on the receiving end? So, I went in search of right-backs who, in truth, were as likely to remember kicking Geordie as much as tackling him – if they were quick enough of course!

PETER RODRIGUES

The first right-back I caught up with was Peter Rodrigues. Peter is perhaps most famous for captaining Southampton to FA Cup victory over the might of Manchester United in 1976, when the Saints were in the old Second Division. However, in a career that saw him earn 40 Welsh caps, Rodrigues also played for Cardiff, Leicester and Sheffield Wednesday, before moving to Southampton. His career spanned from 1961 to 1977, an era during which he played against Geordie on many occasions.

Having faced Geordie for Leicester, Wednesday and the Saints, I asked Peter where he would place the Arsenal winger amongst all the opponents he'd played against and what particular attributes made Geordie the great winger he was?

"I rated him very highly. He was very direct, fast down the wing and didn't 'mess about' like other wingers – George just headed for goal or the goal line to whip in a telling cross."

"George would always put you on edge as a full-back as, apart from being very direct, he had the ability as a winger to go either side of you – not many wingers at the time were good enough to cut inside you, but Geordie certainly was."

I asked if there were any particular memories or matches that stood out whilst playing against Geordie and the Arsenal?

"Although we played against each other several times, the game I recall best was a charity match at Leicester, a Sixties v Seventies all stars match. We had a lot of fun and, as he knocked the ball past me, he'd say "your turn next Pete"... I was famous for sliding tackles, so when I used one on him soon afterwards, I retorted "Okay Geordie, your turn again next!"

"He was very much an unsung hero and a great team player for the Arsenal. George was just such a nice person to be in the company of – a lovely man."

TERRY DARRACOTT

I was fortunate to speak with Terry Darracott, a player who took over from World Cup winner Ray Wilson as Everton right-back in the early Seventies. Terry spent 13 years at Goodison Park as a player, and helped coach the Toffees during the club's mid-Eighties halcyon days. Terry also has a special reason to remember Geordie.

"My first memory of George Armstrong is a happy one as Arsenal were the opponents for my Everton first team debut at Goodison in September 1968 aged 17. I was still an apprentice and it was an unbelievable, unforgettable personal achievement".

Harry Catterick, the Everton manager at the time, had watched Terry play for the youth team the previous week, at right back, and called him up for the only game he played that season because of an injury to Ray Wilson. On the day Terry was asked to play left-back instead because George was playing right wing and vividly remember being briefed beforehand about George Armstrong's threat.

"I was told that by the manager that George was a different kind of winger to the ones I'd encountered so far. Many wingers flitted in an out of games, waiting to receive the ball to sparkle, but George had much more to his game and would get forward to get crosses in, then get back to support his full-back." Terry went on to explain that a full-back would always know they were in for a game when they played against George Armstrong because he was one of the fittest players in the League and they got no rest for the whole 90 minutes.

It was clear from hearing Terry's voice that he had the upmost respect for Geordie as an opponent, sentiments that were encapsulated when he said:

"One thing that was certain with George – you always knew he would take you on and, even if it was not working for him on any given day, he would never stop trying. In George's mind his job for Arsenal was to beat the full-back and get a decent cross in, and that is just what he did – throughout a fantastic career."

I asked Terry why he though Geordie had been overlooked by England. He felt it was simply a case that Sir Alf Ramsey had found a system without wingers, which had worked in 1966, and had stuck with it. He pointed out that both Peter Thompson and Ian Callaghan of Liverpool were selected for squads, but seldom got a game, and concluded by saying that nobody involved in the game at the time would have been surprised if George had played for his country... "He would have done a superb job for England."

ALEX FORSYTH

The perspective offered by Alex is even more valuable when you consider that before returning to his native Scotland in 1968 to join Partick Thistle, he was an apprentice at Arsenal. After establishing himself at Firhill, Alex spent four seasons at Manchester United between 1972 and 1976, and made more than 100 appearances for the Red Devils. But the knowledge gleaned from his time at Highbury certainly didn't made marking 'Wee Geordie' any easier?

The first thing, which comes as no real surprise, is that Geordie, an estab-lished first team regular at Arsenal, went out of his way to make time to chat and assist the young trainees. He gave a young Alex Forsyth coaching on the best body stance, sideways on, to face a tricky winger, who could go both ways, but always gave up time with the apprentices.

"The thing with Geordie was, once he had beaten you, he was away to the bye-line and whipping in a cross. There was no fancy stuff, he wasn't one of those players that would try to beat the fullback more than once. He had everything: pace, superb close control, unparalleled crossing ability with either foot and tracked back"

"Geordie also had a great enthusiasm and a never say die attitude, it was so hard to defend against – not only could he beat you either side, he could also deliver a perfect ball with left of right.

Alex recalls that Bertie Mee also had a strong work ethic and understands exactly why a player like Geordie was always the first name he wrote on his Arsenal team sheet. "George was quite simply the best two-footed winger of his generation – bar none."

Geordie flying down the wing

JOHN MARSH

Another player to have made his debut against a Geordie Armstrong inspired Arsenal side was John Marsh, who was first called into the Stoke starting XI and faced the Gunners on the opening day of the 1967/68 season – he recalls that unlike many wingers, or wide midfielders, who would drift inside, Geordie stayed out wide that match.

It was fascinating to hear the views of the Stoke right-back, who during the epic FA Cup semi-final and replay and two League fixtures, got very well acquainted with Geordie during that Double season. Marsh was ever-present for Stoke City in 1970/71 and, in a 12-year career between 1967-1979; he places George Armstrong among the top six left-wingers he faced.

The irony, which is not lost on John, was that Stoke's best performance that season was a 5-0 drubbing of Arsenal in September, which he describes as the best game he ever played in, but rather than dampen Arsenal's spirit, the drubbing sparked a 14 game unbeaten run.

"There was no respite against the Arsenal and George Armstrong. You always knew you had been in a game – you could never switch off or relax for a minute."

Marsh recalls Geordie's greatest asset, aside from his work-rate, was his ability with either foot, which meant that as a full-back he never knew which way he would try and take you on.

"What you did know, thought, was that Geordie would try and take you on and get a cross in and with the calibre of strikers that Arsenal possessed that season, both such great headers of the ball, you had to try and stop the supply line."

Of course, with Geordie, this was easier said than done, but Marsh recalls with some wingers you could 'make your presence felt' in the first ten minutes or so, which could make them think twice before taking you on but, that wasn't the case with all players it would appear. "George could not be intimidated; he would just come back for more."

Marsh suggested that with George's box-to-box ability he could have easily played the role Alan Ball did for England and there was little to choose between the two ability-wise. Ironically, they ended up as teammates and close friends – Bally won 72 caps for England versus Geordie's none.

"Well I can't speak for Sir Alf Ramsey, but the biggest compliment I can pay is that everybody at Stoke City would have a loved a George Armstrong in our team, and I suspect every team in the land at that time would have said the same."

GEORGE COHEN

Finally, and arguably most notably, I was fortunate to be able to speak to the one and only World Cup winning right-back, George Cohen. The England and Fulham legend was only too delighted to respond to my written request for an interview and I was left in no illusion that he would not have shared his memories for many. "I would not have bothered to call for just anyone, but I thought a great deal of George Armstrong."

Cohen, who would have faced Geordie between 1962 and 1968, the year when Fulham were relegated to the second-tier, described how fast George was, and how everything was executed with such a pace and supreme balance. Like so many great players, who perhaps aren't the tallest, possessing a low centre of gravity and smaller step, often heightens the balance and enhances ball control. So, in that respect, George likened Geordie to Puskas and Garrincha. High praise indeed.

Cohen echoes the sentiment that with Geordie you were in a game for 90 minutes and he gave an opponent "not a moment's rest". The Craven Cottage favourite had also build his game on speed and loved to attack down the wing, so the battle between the two Georges took place from one end of the pitch to the other. Cohen says he always tried to show Geordie the outside but wryly admits that his adversary would not always do what he wanted and concluded with a lovely line. "The fans would have a loved a player like George Armstrong because he never cheated the game."

And who are we to argue with a World Cup Winner?

THE JOURNALISTS' MATCH REPORTS

If we are to achieve a fully 360-degree perspective on George Armstrong, I felt it would be appropriate to collect the opinions of the 'gentlemen of the Press' – those who were paid to write about our beautiful game at the time. We have all got frustrated with football journalists at one time or another through their written words, or the views offered through radio or television broadcasts, but none of us would question, I suspect, their love of football, or indeed those who practice the game's art well. There may be occasions, however, where may doubt the impartiality of ex-players as pundits, but I take the view that if a journalist or pundit was watching Geordie at his peak for the Arsenal, their non-partisan views still have a huge merit and I was extremely fortunate to be able to speak with some of the best football scribes of that era.

Five-times winner of the prestigious 'Sports Journalist of the Year' award, Patrick is a hugely respected columnist who began reporting on top-flight football in the late Sixties – just as Bertie Mee's Arsenal were coming to the fore. Patrick recalls Armstrong as being totally integral to the way Arsenal played and, amusingly, his first reflection was about how much quicker he was than perhaps he initially looked.

He also felt that although Geordie has always been regarded as a firm fans favourite for his work rate and selflessness, this perhaps overshadowed his immense talent; "In reality I think that whenever you mention the Double side, fans often remember lesser players than Geordie first."

He mused that it may have been Geordie's selflessness and modesty that worked against him in that respect but, equally, he knew the man himself would not have cared a single jot – "Geordie was understated and never pushed himself to the fore – he was simply not concerned about his own profile and just wanted to play football."

"He was undeniably influential to the great Arsenal side and, with two great headers of the ball in Radford and Kennedy, Geordie's crossing was critical to the success of the team. I can still see him now, scuttling up and down the left touchline."

It is fair to say that journalists in those days could be paid almost as much as the players themselves, as well as enjoying enormous Fleet Street expense accounts – but Geordie was not one to drink with the Press or go out for a meal, as Collins recalls; "He was far more likely to have one and then be off home to his family – Geordie always struck me as an uncomplicated man with no side to him and not attracted to the celebrity lifestyle of being a footballer."

Collins agreed that Geordie was always likely to beat his full-back, and added some superb insight into how he was often the catalyst for Arsenal breakaway attacks; "Geordie was Arsenal's outlet when clearing their lines. He never failed to receive the ball, then skip the first challenge in his own half, before setting off on the offensive – either alone, or through an incisive pass to a team mate."

It is always said in football that the great players know what they are going to do with the ball before they receive it, as Collins underlines; "Truly great players always manage to translate the picture in their mind into reality on the field of play, and Geordie was a master of that art. It was when Geordie received the ball that things tended to happen for the Arsenal."

Collins concluded by underpinning Geordie's attributes simply and beautifully; "George Armstrong was the ordinary bloke next door with an extraordinary talent. His sudden passing, at such a young age, was a tragic loss to football – he was so hugely respected by everyone in the game."

Norman has written more football books than some of us have eaten healthy meals, in truth, far too many of them have been about Arsenal's North London neighbours, however, from 1964 to 1974 he was the Daily Express football correspondent for London. In short he watched and reported on Geordie at his absolute peak for a decade and few are better qualified to provide a neutral, yet expert, perspective. "Geordie was the thinking man's winger – fleet of foot, strong on the ball and deadly accurate with his crosses and corner kicks."

He recollects how Armstrong always positioned himself intelligently, always available to receive the ball from Bob Wilson, or collect a well-directed clearance without the opposition catching on to the fact they were about to fall victim of a cleverly rehearsed ploy. This concurs with Patrick Collins assertion that it was Geordie who was the main protagonist when it came to transforming defence to attack for the Gunners.

"George was an unselfish player who always put the team ahead of any personal glory and, more often than not, when I was writing up my notes for a match report, a close analysis of goal-scoring moves usually revealed that it was Armstrong who had played a crucial 'assist' role somewhere along the way."

"In his 500 League matches for the Gunners, George must have run the equivalent of a hundred marathons – his work rate was astonishing, and he always went about his work with enthusiasm and energy."

When I asked if any particular matches stood out in his memory, Norman recites the night Arsenal went to Tottenham for their final League game of the 1970/71 season. North London derbies are always tense occasions, but this one carried the extra dynamite that a Gunners victory would hand them the First Division title. George, as usual, played with total commitment, and set up the vital headed goal for Ray Kennedy that clinched the Championship – it was an unforgettable night for the North East boys in North London.

"What a season that was for George. He was an ever-present in the team that won the League and FA Cup double, the architect of so many vital goals."

Arsenal had infamously gone 17 years without winning a trophy when they took on Anderlecht in the Fairs Cup Final in 1969/70 and Armstrong was to be instrumental in ending that dismal run. I asked for Norman's thoughts about that two-legged Fairs Cup triumph, which so many commentators have describe as Geordie's finest hour.

"George wore the number seven shirt but kept switching wings as he ran himself into the ground over the two legs. Arsenal were three goals down in Belgium and looked dead and buried, but George conjured a late opening for Ray Kennedy, the new kid on the block, who snatched the goal that gave them a life-line and some hope in the return leg."

Giller travelled home with the team and recalls how George's was among the loudest voices on the trip back to London, insisting they could still win the cup.

"George was here, there and everywhere in the second leg and it was unanimously felt among his team-mates that he was the unheralded man of the match – the Gunners pulled off an incredible Cup-winning victory to end all those years of Arsenal misery – a barren spell that, as a closet Tottenham supporter, had pleased me!"

Giller is as bemused as everyone else that Geordie's club excellence was not rewarded by an England call-up – he feels Geordie was desperately unlucky not to get that recognition. "Sadly he had his peak seasons just as Alf Ramsey was conquering the world with his Wingless Wonders but I remember Don Howe telling me "Alf would be doing himself and England a favour by picking George. He would be the ideal linking man for his 4-3-3 formation because he does the work of two men. "Even though 1966 had been too early for George, I was amazed that he didn't make Ramsey's 28-man squad for the trip to Mexico for the 1970 World Cup, which was eventually trimmed to 22. Geordie would have been perfect for the work rate that was required in the sapping heat."

Whilst researching and writing this book, and through speaking to so many who knew Geordie personally, I feel I have come, in some way, to know the man so well – but the following quote from Norman Giller is amongst my favourite and epitomizes the man's modest nature: "George's next boast would have been his first."

"Geordie was always first to the bar, and would be jumping in to buy the next round, too. He could sink a beer or three, but was never out of order and knew when to stop... well, most of the time!"

He was, according to Giller, generous with both his money and his time, and was always looking out for young Ray Kennedy, a fellow Geordie, who was still learning the ropes. The trait of wanting to help others was a constant theme through his career. "In short, he was a good man, and once you had won his confidence, he became a friend for life."

In asking for any personal anecdotes, Giller was able to clear up what, for me, was an anomaly to a degree. Overwhelmingly we have the impression of a modest, hard-working man, who just felt blessed to be a footballer. The flashiness and lifestyle associated were not for Geordie, although he did have lovely cars.

Giller remembers how Geordie was the talk of Arsenal after turning up for training one day in a sleek new Jaguar, which was completely out of character at the time. "He gave me a lift into town from the London Colney training ground one afternoon and Geordie turned to me and said, "I hope you don't think I'm being flash. It's always been my dream to have a Jag. Not bad for a working-class kid from Hebburn who was meant to be an electrician. This is all due to football." And no, Norman didn't think he was being flash. "It was typical of George, that he felt almost embarrassed to be driving such an expensive,

high-powered car [pictured left] in the days before players were earning huge amounts. I was thrilled for him. He's earned that right."

BRIAN JAMES   DAILY MAIL

Brian covered top-flight football for the Daily Mail from the late Fifties until the mid-Seventies and remembers Geordie Armstrong very fondly. When I asked Brian to describe Geordie as a footballer he told me that journalists obviously love to use many words, and long ones at that, but, in this instance, he thought three would suffice. "Fast and tricky!"

"He was the sort of winger that gave a fullback no rest at all for the full length of the game – he would run and run – he never stopped trying to take them on. The opposition could not take their eyes of him – he was forever on the move, and because he was so two-footed, they could be exposed on the outside or inside. On top of that, it was even worse playing against Geordie because the customary 'good kick to let him know you were there' did not work. Armstrong would simply get up and smile, as if to say 'is that the best you've got?'"

According to James, when things were not going well and the team was losing, when others' heads might have dropped, or players could have gone into their shells, Geordie would do the opposite. "He would double his effort and encourage his team mates to do the same. Every manager would have wanted a George Armstrong in their team and his name would have been the first on their team sheets."

James has an interesting take on why Geordie did not get a look in for England and the facts seem to back up his argument. "Ramsey had four out-and-out wingers in the 1966 World Cup squad, but none of them were considered to have performed in the early games in the tournament by the national team manager. Both John Connelly of Manchester United (Uruguay), and Ian Callaghan of Liverpool (France), were given a game but hadn't delivering to Ramsay's satisfaction it seemed – Southampton's Terry Paine also played in one match (Mexico). For Paine and Connelly their game in 1966 were to be their last – Ramsey deciding that Martin Peters and Alan Ball were to be the winning formula. It was that combination, certainly not Armstrong's ability, which ultimately prevented George getting the call-up that so many in the game felt he deserved."

Journalists would all wait patiently in the Marble Halls at Highbury after a match, waiting for the players to come out, and hoping to grab a brief interview or a quote or two. Some players would walk past with a wave of the hand, but not Geordie, who would always stop and talk. James recalls that it never seemed like George was doing it out of a duty or obligation. "It was as if Geordie felt that you had watched him enjoy doing his job and he was happy to help us do ours. He treated everyone as an equal, Geordie would not have to be asked to chat, he would stop and say, 'So, what did you think of the game Brian?' He would do the same with other journalists and then he would spend time outside signing autographs for the fans."

"It seemed that, for Geordie, every day was like living a dream – being paid for being a footballer and doing the things he loved the most – the giving of his time, whether it be to fans, colleagues or journalists, was seen as giving something back and was the most natural thing in the world to the player."

MARTIN TYLER   SKY SPORTS

To most people, for the last 20 years or so, Martin Tyler's voice is an instantly recognisable part of the match-day output of Sky Sports, but he was a football writer before his switch to TV. Tyler's first position as a football journalist was on the *Book of Football* in 1971 – Brian James was the Consulting Editor of a weekly publication, which built into a book through instalments. It was a memorable first week at work for young Martin – in fact his very first day was the Monday that Arsenal clinched the League at White Hart Lane and, the following Saturday, the Double was completed at Wembley.

However, as a student in Sixties London, when not playing himself, Tyler had been a regular visitor to Highbury – so his admiration for Armstrong long-preceded any professional interest. Tyler, who played to a fairly decent standard himself, admits he always appreciated Armstrong's work rate and energy, and describes the Arsenal legend as "Even more wholehearted then the definition of wholehearted states in the dictionary, if that is possible? George must have been a dream for his team mates and his manager, but it was not just the quantity of the work with Geordie, but the quality too."

Tyler feels that Arsenal team of 1971 has been described by some as being rather functional, but to him, it was more an efficient system that brought success. "Get the ball to Geordie, he will deliver with precision and Radford or Kennedy would get on the end of it. There was always another player competing for your place in a selection of only 12, so the fact that he was an ever-present for so many years is testament to his quality – he brought so much to the team. Nobody could have taken his place."

"One of the joys of football is that a team needs selfless workers to play alongside those who catch the eye with exceptional talents. Geordie Armstrong was one of a rare breed who encapsulated both categories. The perfect team man with match winning qualities as well." On the subject of functionality versus flair, Tyler concurs with Brain James when it comes to the international

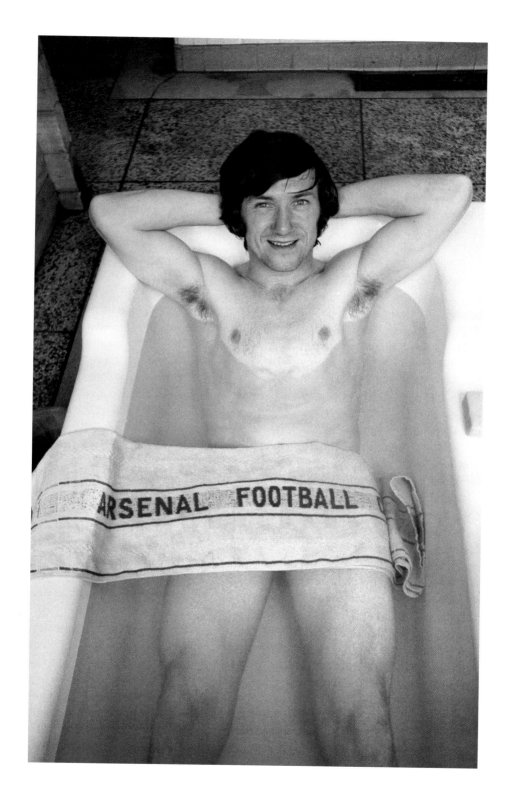

recognition that eluded Geordie, however, he does not recall a single interview or conversation he had with the man where he ever complained or pushed himself to the fore in a quest to win a cap for England. "He was too modest and just proud to be playing for the Arsenal."

When Tyler first made the move to television it was working behind the scenes on the production team of the *Big Match* and *On the Ball* for ITV and was, in his own words, a 'nobody' in the terms of the show's hierarchy, but not to Geordie. "He would talk to me as if I was the most important person in his life at that moment. We had many conversations in which Geordie would happily chat about football for ages and I'm still struck by the time a star footballer was willing to give to a junior journalist making his way in television." The key, of course, was that Geordie Armstrong did not consider himself a star, just an ordinary bloke who could play a bit.

Tyler collaborated with Phil Soar on *The Official History of Arsenal* by writing the post-war section, and in doing so, had cause to interview Armstrong – but it was later, when Geordie was back at the club post-1990, that he truly got to know Armstrong and was fortunate to be able to spend time at the Arsenal training ground. Even if he was busy coaching, Geordie would wave from the pitch. Often the two men would sit in the coach's hut drinking tea and discussing Arsenal, or wider points in the game – "Geordie always had an opinion backed with a deep knowledge and thoughtfulness about the game he loved. There was nothing contrived about Geordie – his charm was natural. There was no doubt in my mind exactly why Geordie was such a respected coach or why players of all ages and experience would gladly work with him."

"He would have been embarrassed to hear the word 'charisma' used about himself, but he had it in natural abundance. He would look you in the eyes and he spoke to you from the heart."

Back in 1973, at the very start of his television career, Tyler was aware that there was an 'Arsenal Way' of doing things and an expected standard of behaviour; "George Armstrong epitomised all that was good about Arsenal and football. He represented the club admirably as a player and later as a coach, understanding the joy of being a footballer but, at the same time, respecting the privilege of being given that opportunity. I witnessed him pass on that knowledge and understanding to future stars, who absorbed that wisdom and improved as players as a result."

We can also be in little doubt on the impact that Geordie had on Tyler personally. "Nobody deserves this tribute more than Geordie. He was the salt of the earth. In all my time in football no-one has made more of an impression – he was just so endearing and special."

In summarising these various conversations, and the countless observations of Geordie from his many admirers, sometimes one quote simply screams out to be used in this book – however, this last paragraph was directly taken from a letter that Martin Tyler sent me, rather than from my initial interview.

Our conversation had obviously got him thinking more about Armstrong. "I got to know George personally in the Eighties, a friendship that I cherished. In a busy life, he always had time for a chat. Football was never just a job for him. It was a way of life and you could sense how grateful he was for the game being good to him. It was a two-way street because George Armstrong was great for the game. I was very proud to have known him."

STEVE STAMMERS   SUNDAY MIRROR

Steve Stammers will be known to most as an old school journalist at the Mirror and the author of *Arsenal: The Official Biography - The Compelling Story of an Amazing Club*. It was, however, back in 1973 when Stammers began reporting on the London football world, writing for the now defunct London Evening News.

Geordie was still at his peak at the time, even if the Arsenal team itself was not quite reaching its previous heights and it was clear to Stammers how every team in the land would have been envious of Arsenal for having Armstrong in their side. "He was reliable and dependable, hard working beyond belief and integral to the Arsenal system – the side relied heavily on him. Armstrong was a top player who never sought any publicity or was involved in any controversy. All the headlines about Geordie were for football reasons – he was a thoroughly decent man on and of the pitch."

"I don't recall him ever being injured, or complaining about being continually fouled, which he undoubtedly was – he was a thoroughly tough little bugger!" Stammers believes that Geordie was a player ahead of his time, a box-to-box winger so unlike most in that era, and a player who truly came alive with the ball at his feet. "George was a working winger, not a posing winger."

"In many ways George was representative of Bertie Mee's successful team – on paper the eleven individuals should not have made a great Double winning team perhaps, but because they functioned so well as together they became one. George Armstrong was the side's essence and oil in that Arsenal machine."

"He always had time to talk to the reporters after a match, and would often, inadvertently, give us a headline story after speaking so thoughtfully and knowledgeably about the game. It was no surprise that he became such a respected coach later in his career."

Stammers also remembered the sense of complete shock when George passed away so suddenly – after all, that devastating news came shortly after Arsene Wenger had commented on how fit Armstrong had looked whilst watching him train at full pace with the reserves 35 years his junior – the Arsenal manager had joked that, as he had so many injuries, he was thinking of putting George on the bench for the first team. "George was a delightful, positive,

A rare sight – an injured George Armstrong

thinking man – he always spoke like he played – honest, straight and absolutely dedicated to the Arsenal."

My aim in writing this chapter was, primarily, to illicit some insight from those who watched and wrote about Geordie at his best, however, whilst making contact with the Mirror's senior statesman, Steve Stammers, one of the newspaper's younger band of writers was keen add his tribute as to Armstrong's memory.

John worked his way up to the nationals after starting his scribe's 'apprenticeship' aged 17 on his local paper, The Islington Gazette, in 1988. His father had been brought up on Blackstock Road so, in truth, there was only ever one team in the Cross household and he recalls his dad always going on and on about Geordie Armstrong from a fairly young age. Cross was first taken to Highbury in 1975/76 and, of course, Geordie was one of the senior statesmen in that Arsenal team.

"If I'm being honest I don't recall Geordie as a player so much, but Armstrong really struck a chord with me when I was a young reporter when I was regularly writing about Arsenal and doing bits for the match day programme."

"I spent a lot of time at the training ground in 1990 and I got to know quite a few of the figures – George Graham was good to me – but the one person who really stood out was George Armstrong, who, to this day, remains one of the nicest people I have ever come across in football."

John Cross will always remember going to reserve and youth team games at Highbury, or Colney, where Geordie always knew that he was there, then came to find him. "We would have a few words about the game, then would just talk and talk about football in general. I was just a young kid in my early 20's, so it was an amazing experience and I felt he was making a real fuss of me." Geordie knew that Cross was keen to learn and was more than happy to adopt the role of teacher, often correcting the young writer on observations he had made.

"My football knowledge increased hugely through my discussions with Geordie, he'd listen to what I said without ever patronising me and, for that, I will be eternally grateful."

"After a little while Geordie would insist on giving me a lift home – very few people were allowed at the training ground back then, probably just the local paper and the programme staff, so it could be intimidating for a novice reporter, but Geordie would always make us feel welcome. George Graham was also very approachable, but Geordie would always invite me into the Coach's room for chats that would often go on for ages. In fact, on one occasion, Pat Rice and Steve Rowley had left us talking before heading off on a scouting mission to watch John Hartson at Luton. When they returned, several hours later, they were astonished to find us still sat where we had been hours earlier, still talking. I owe George so much, he was simply different class!"

THE TESTIMONIAL YEAR: 1974

I n the spring of 1974, just three weeks after his 500th appearance for the Arsenal first team – an occasion marked by the presentation of a silver cannon – the club welcomed Barcelona to Highbury to play in Geordie's testimonial match, it was a Barca side that included somebody who is still regarded as possibly the World's greatest player, the mercurial Johan Cruyff.

Arsenal had played against Cruyff on four occasions in fairly quick succession at that time – as captain of Ajax, when Arsenal had got the better of the Dutch giants over two legs in the Fairs Cup Semi-Final in 1970; then losing in the 1972 European Cup Quarter-Final. Charlie George told me that he felt a mutual respect had built between the two combatants and, he was certain, that Cruyff had considerable individual regard for the talent of Geordie Armstrong.

There was a curious backdrop to the testimonial, which was the second friendly match against the Catalans in the season. Whilst Cruyff had been signed in mid August 1973, there had been some bureaucratic issues between Ajax and Barcelona and, as a result, he was not eligible to make his debut for his new club until October 23rd. Prior to this, as Bob Wilson recalled, Barca had invited Arsenal to play a competitive friendly at the Neu Camp to assist them integrate the Dutchman and bolster his match fitness. It would be an attractive fixture and pull a large crowd due to the prestigious nature of the English visitors.

Arsenal agreed, but the way Wilson recalls it, the Arsenal board stipulated a condition – that Barcelona, with Johan Cruyff and a full strength side, returned the favour the following spring for Geordie Armstrong's testimonial game. Arsenal secured the biggest name and draw in world football for their loyal winger's big night.

A notable aside is that by playing, and losing 1-0 in the Neu Camp friendly, Armstrong and his Arsenal team mates actually played in Cruyff's first ever appearance in an Barcelona shirt. He was to play one more friendly, against Club Deportivo Ourense on October 20, before scoring a brace in his competitive debut against Getafe three days later.

Of course, the Arsenal team of 1974 were not performing at the same heights they had been a few years earlier, and the testimonial was ultimately an easy 3-1 victory for Barcelona [pictured left], but that was not the point. The night, and the match, was all about two men – Geordie Armstrong and Johan Cruyff. The Dutch maestro was a crowd puller, whilst Geordie was a firm home fans' favourite – the combination should have ensured a superb crowd to bolster the testimonial fund of a Gunner legend – and it did.

Arsenal were a team in transition, languishing mid table and, as a consequence, the weekly attendance for home games had dipped below 30,000 for the first times in years. It was not the case on the evening of March 12 however, when over 36,000 fans paid their 50 pence at the Highbury turnstiles to cheer on a Gunners stalwart whilst expecting to be dazzled by the skills of Cruyff.

A young Liam Brady proudly lined up alongside his mentor and friend and recalls what a massive accolade it was to get so many in for a friendly testimonial. He was not surprised though, he knew just how much Geordie was respected and loved by the Arsenal faithful and that was perfectly reflected in the clicks at the gates.

"The lofty genius of Johan Cruyff and the more homely virtues of the loyal, dependable George Armstrong, drew a 36,099 crowd into Highbury last night for the little winger's testimonial..." was the lead paragraph in the Daily Express the following morning. They went on to report... "Cruyff, who when playing in earnest, is said to earn a cool £100 a minute, politely gave us 70 minutes for nothing."

Geordie was joined in the Arsenal line up that evening by many of his closest friends: Wilson, Rice, Simpson, Storey, Ball, Brady and Kennedy all started for his Arsenal that evening and, even though the occasion ended in defeat, its main objective was to pay tribute and to reward Geordie for his service to the club – in that respect it was a complete success.

The following morning, Geoffrey Green, writing for The Times, reported about those financial reward for Armstrong; "The attendance he was happy enough to learn was over 36,000; when expenses are paid to the visitor, little Armstrong should feel that his 13 years with the club has not gone unrewarded. He deserves every penny. His drive and enthusiasm apart, he, like only a handful of others, has been a model and an example to the modern game."

So where exactly had the evolution of 'the modern game' reached in 1974 and where did Geordie feel he fitted into the hierarchy of football? Reproduced with the kind permission of Arsenal Football Club, Armstrong's personal introduction to his testimonial programme offers an insightful snapshot into his mind-set at that time of his career.

"Sometimes, when I am thinking about the success I have enjoyed in football, I think of the people who have helped me get there. I shall always think of Vic Groves. I lived with Vic and his wife when I first came to Highbury, thirteen years ago, and Vic had a great influence on my career. He had a great love for the game, total dedication, he was able to discipline himself (and me too!) and I suppose you could say his influence moulded me for the future. He was like a big brother and I shall always be grateful to him. I am grateful too to Dave Sexton and Don Howe and indeed, to Bertie Mee, for whom I have great respect. I would like to mention George Swindin, who made up his mind about me when I came to Highbury for a trial. It was a great ordeal for me. How different everything was from what I had been used to. It was George's kindness that made me certain that I wanted to sign for Arsenal. For me there is no other club."

"Yes, things have changed a great deal since I started here. The success of England in the World Cup in 1966, with England playing in a certain way, was the start of a complete change round in football tactics. If you don't give goals away – then you can't lose. That is the basis of it all and, in my opinion, it has spoiled football, as you have all seen, when a team comes to Highbury for a point. In the old days the orthodox winger's game was to take on and beat the full-back. If he did, then you might create a scoring chance. Today you are not confronted by one full-back. You have a whole line of players falling back and there is a mass of players in the penalty area. These defensive tactics do not give players the chance to show their skill – the sort of skills you see from them in training."

Armstrong and Cruyff:
Mutual respect from the world's finest

The Armstrongs with The Mees

Geordie's thoughts from forty-plus years ago are still echoed by Arsenal supporters regarding the spoilers of attacking, enterprising football at The Emirates – and it is perhaps why so many of his colleagues feel Armstrong would fit seamlessly into a modern Wenger side. The tradition of 4-4-2, with one orthodox winger and one box-to-box midfielder, had been utilised by both Graham and Wenger in the years since Geordie ceased to play for Arsenal, but, truth is, Armstrong could have excelled in either role or, indeed, both. He could have been Marwood, or Limpar, or Overmars – he could also have been Rocastle or Parlour.

Geordie concluded his programme notes; "Can I end these few thoughts by thanking everyone for the support you have given me over the years? Thank you for coming tonight and thank you to all those of you who have been close to the arrangements for this game. You have all been terrific and you know how grateful I am to you and to Arsenal. Arsenal has been my life."

Not only was there to be a testimonial match to mark Geordie's consistency and longevity of service to Arsenal, but a Gala celebration dinner and ball was held at the Grosvenor Hotel, which was organised by Eric Morley. Morley, with his wife Julia, was perhaps best known for his organisation of the annual Miss World pageant, but his company, Mecca, also ran the catering at Highbury. This Gala allowed Geordie and his wife, Marj, to invite their

friends and close family to join the celebrations and to thank them for their support. The event, held on October 20, saw George and Marj greet guests, at the reception *[pictured above]*, followed by dinner, speeches, cabaret, then dancing, with carriages arranged for 2am.

Geordie's guests were entertained by Lovelace Watkins, the Las Vegas based crooner, nicknamed 'The Black Sinatra' and danced to band leader Ray McVay and Andy Ross with their respective orchestras. Among the family guests were Edward Armstrong, Geordie's father, sisters Agnes and Ellen and Marj's parents and sisters, their spouses and her brother.

Billy Wright, Geordie's second Arsenal manager, along with Joy Beverly of the Beverley Sisters, and Bertie Mee and his wife Doris were also present, as were most of his team mates and their wives. Making up the impressive who's who were ex-colleagues and footballing peers – the Arsenal board was represented by Dennis Hill-Wood and Ken Friar and their partners. Both the club and the supporters had prepared a special message for Geordie in the event programme;

From Arsenal; "Our good wishes to Geordie for a great evening and an even greater future from everyone at Arsenal." From the fans; "Arsenal Football Supporter's Club send best wishes to George for a successful evening and thank him for all the pleasure he has given us over the years."

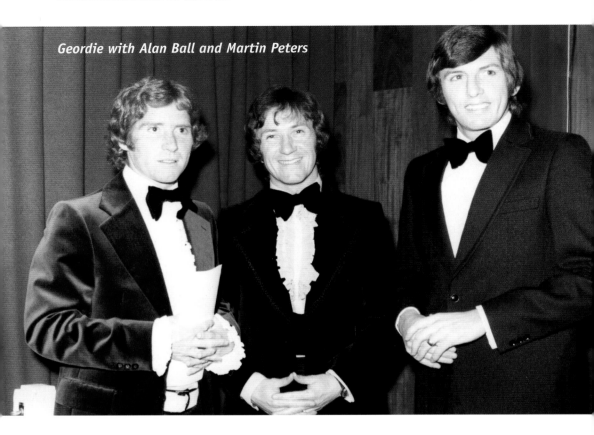

Geordie with Alan Ball and Martin Peters

When it was time for Geordie to make his speech he thanked the Testimonial Committee, the organisers, his guest and of course his family, but a special mention was reserved for his father, Edward. Sadly, his mother had died in the late Sixties and had not lived to see her son lift the trophies he did with Arsenal, but his father had always been there for him and was a great believer in his ability.

Geordie, clearly moved, thanked his dad for everything but, with typical humour, observed "You probably won't be able to see him because he is so small, even smaller then me!" On hearing this, and unprompted, Edward rose from his table and walked to the top table to greet his son *[pictured]*, to shake his hand, and share the proud moment. There was not a dry eye in the Great Ballroom after that!

Both events were wonderful tributes to one of Arsenal's own, who had served the club with distinction through bad times and good, great disappointments and greater glories. A player who had reinvented the word enthusiasm when it came to playing the game he loved and whose work-rate and dynamism had made him the envy of manager, team and supporters across the land. A footballer appreciated by the whole of English football it seemed – but not by the manager of the England team!

Geordie with his dad – there was not a dry eye in the Great Ballroom

On that note, one of the final photographs in this chapter, taken at the Grosvenor Gala evening, is of Geordie with team mate, Alan Ball, and another England World Cup Winner and friend, Martin Peters, which I find mildly ironic. To see our hero smiling with the two men, who arguably prevented him winning any international recognition with England, the left and right midfielders in a successful three-man midfield, which Alf Ramsey employed for nine years – without wingers. What's even more ironic is that both Ball and Peters thought their manager was wrong to ignore the talents of Armstrong.

I know from speaking with so many other Arsenal players that Ball felt his friend should have been in the England squads of the early 1970s, having played against Geordie for Everton, then alongside him at Arsenal. Peters, too, once selected an England XI that included an uncapped Geordie so I am told – Armstrong and Peters having made their England Under-18 debuts together in the spring of 1962.

A shame then, that the England captain of 1973 and the England Captain of 1975, pictured at a tribute to their good friend and fellow professional at his testimonial dinner in 1974, did not hold more sway with Sir Alf!

A NORTH BANK HERO: THE FANS' TRIBUTE

The respect for Geordie's ability as a footballer from his peers, both team mates and opponents, will be obvious to you having read this far – colleagues have spoken ebulliently about his enthusiasm, his selflessness, his work-rate, his natural fitness and, of course, his mercurial talent and wing-play.

However, as this whole book is a tribute to Geordie, and whilst it is wonderful to hear about the man from those who played with him, it is equally important to give a voice to those who paid their heard-earned cash, week in and week out, to watch their Gunners heroes. For many, as we will discover, George 'Geordie' Armstrong was one of those heroes and a player that still has a special place in the hearts of so many, almost 40 years since he last pulled on the club's red and white shirt in anger.

For me, as a ten-year-old, I saw him play twice at Highbury during the 1976/77 season – his final campaign with Arsenal. Even then I was an avid reader of football annuals such as *Shoot* and *Roy of the Rovers*, as well as watching Arsenal on the football highlights shows *Big Match* and *Match Of The Day*. I could name all the players from the Double winning side and I knew on that crisp September's day, when the staring eleven were named, there remained two of those history-making Gunners in the side. Despite the team boasting the (then) England captain, Alan Ball, and the recent record signing, Malcolm Macdonald, in attack, the real Arsenal legends were Peter Simpson and George Armstrong. I remember Geordie being everywhere, taking corners, a free kick that just failed to creep under the bar, bursting runs. But the sad reality is that I would feel a fraud if I contributed to this tribute in earnest. No, that privilege has to fall to those who are a little older than me perhaps, and were fortunate enough to have witnessed first hand Geordie at his peak, all over the land. We start by reproducing two letters sent to Jill Armstrong shortly after her father left us in 2000.

My first memory of your dad was from a child's perspective, when I finally fulfilled my childhood dream and got to Highbury in the early Seventies. We sat very close to the touchline and this mercurial figure, with his socks rolled down and George Best hair, shot past us, beat two tackles and knocked in a perfect cross. I asked who that player was and was told Georgie Armstrong, and I said I want to play like that. Unfortunately the Lord didn't bless me with your father's skills and I became more a Willie Young type player! Please pass my regards to all your family. You should rightly be proud of the enormous pleasure your dad gave to millions of people and how his legacy lives on in hundreds of youngsters who have been inspired and encouraged by him.
Dermot Murnaghan – ITN News Reader

I am honoured to write about such a revered man as the great George Armstrong. He was as much part of Highbury as the Marble Hall itself. The last time I saw him was whilst playing in one of those many five-a-side tournaments at Highbury and I actually got to shake his hand. And I am not ashamed to say that it was one of the greatest thrills for me. I had not seen him for probably 25 years or more and, apart from a few grey hairs (well to be honest a full head of grey hairs), he had not changed a bit. He still seemed to have the same enthusiasm for the game as when I watch him belting down the wing in the Seventies. He was one of the few players that the Arsenal fans genuinely took to their hearts – they truly loved him. He didn't have the fire of Frank McLintock. He wasn't flamboyant like Charlie George – and I hope you are not offended when I say he was not the greatest footballer

Highbury has ever seen – but there was something about the way he played that you just had to enjoy. He was a true entertainer. For a start, he was the player who put the fear of God into the opposing full-back. To see Georgie Armstrong on the ball was a joy and the crowd just loved watching him. If Arsenal were ever struggling, invariably one tactic you would hear from the crowd was; "Give it to Geordie! Give it to Geordie!"

One-on-one there has never been a better player at Highbury – Overmars included. Our money was on George every time. You could feel the tension and anticipation in the crowd rise every time he got the ball. We'd watch him, almost on tiptoes, as he gently teased the defender with the ball then, with perfect timing, he'd pick the exact moment to push the ball past him and down the wing. Then, with a burst of speed Linford Christie would have been proud of, he'd overtake the full-back, race toward the corner flag, and provide the perfect cross for John Radford. When you watched George Armstrong play you watched him with a smile on your face. That is my overriding memory of Geordie.

I didn't know Geordie personally, I only wish I had, for everyone I have every met that knew him speaks of him as 'THE nicest man in football.'
Gary Wilmot – Singer, actor and comedian

I was a nine or ten-year-old when I first discovered the joys of supporting Arsenal Football Club... a passion that has continued 45 years longer than any hobby or relationship I've had other than with my family. And one name synonymous with those early days was Armstrong's. A great name, which to me, as a boy, conjured up an image of a mixture between the cartoon characters Popeye and Road Runner.

His was a consistent name on the team sheet and, as I got to know the personalities and playing styles of the Arsenal team of the late Sixties and Seventies, 'Armstrong' became simply 'Geordie' and one of my firm favourites. A tireless engine who skilfully weaved up and down the flanks delivering pinpoint crosses to other heroes like Radford, Kennedy and Graham.

He also scored some key goals himself, including a great FA Cup semi final goal against Stoke that was watched frame by frame by school kids throughout the land, over and over again – that goal was featured in a 'photo flickbook' as a collectable promotional giveaway by the Daily Mirror.

In the double side of 1971 he was ever-present and represented the gutsy fighting spirit of the Gunners, who came together and created history as a unit – fighting for their triumphs and recognition based on team spirit, hard work and flair.

In 1973/74 he was honoured with a richly deserved testimonial game, following many years of loyal service. The visitors were mighty Barcelona including the Dutch legend Johan Cruyff as captain. How appropriate it was to see the fans come out in their droves to celebrate with, and honour, the hugely popular Arsenal legend that was George Armstrong.

I still have a commemorative pennant from that match and remember also the huge support and accolades from everyone. Geordie, in the famous red and white shirt, received his special silver cannon for notching up his 500th appearance from chairman Sir Dennis Hill-Wood – then went on to become the Arsenal appearance record holder.

In later years, when I became Arsenal's magician, performing pre-match as part of the club's match day hospitality, I met George several times. Geordie had returned to the club on the coaching staff and I was delighted to get to know the man that I had hero worshipped as a kid. I was not disappointed. He was every bit as warm, humble and popular as I could have hoped. I was thrilled to even play a game or two with him with the Arsenal ex-pro Celebrity XI.

George Armstrong is a big part of the Arsenal history and will always be remembered with great affection by everyone. He was a great player, full of passion, and a true gentleman.

Marvin Berglas - Arsenal Match Day Magician

Geordie Armstrong was surely the sort of player every professional enjoys playing alongside. The reason for that is fairly simple, you'd never see him give less than one hundred percent and he always managed to leave the field of play looking as if he'd been locked in a sauna for 90 minutes. At the end of most games George had little, or nothing, left to give, not only did he give his all but his matted, sweaty hair gave honest witness to his endeavours. His work rate was phenomenal and no cause was ever seemingly lost so far as George was concerned. There is one instance I recall, in what was pretty much a 'nothing' game, where his very essence was distilled in a brief cameo.

It was a home match in the late Sixties that was going nowhere, I don't even recall our opponents other than that they were wearing dark striped shirts and the pitch was the normal muddy, wintery mess that had slowed down the match. George did something fairly simple; he chased the ball down as it was passed to one of the other team's midfielders, which made the player hurry and passed it on to a defender – there was no way George would get the ball but he chased it down anyway.

The defender, in turn, cleared the ball away with a thirty-yard pass, but Geordie curved his run to chase down the next man – he was effectively chasing shadows. But the crowd's interest had been aroused and murmured its approval, before waking fully from its slumbers and galvanised some encouraging support for our wee winger. What started as a kind of resurgence of interest transformed into an encouraging roar and crescendoed in rapturous appreciation. In all, I believe there were five consecutive passes that were chased down by the flying Geordie before the almost inevitable error occurred when another Arsenal player, clearly encouraged by George's madness, got in first to intercept the next pass. It's the little moments that can change matches, and this whole-hearted little man had changed the match and the crowd's attitude to the game.

Geordie chased down another seemingly lost cause at White Hart Lane in the 87th minute of the game played on May 3, 1971 – a moment that not only changed a match but also footballing history – it was no coincidence that it was wee Geordie who chased and recovered that particular ball towards the end of a mentally and physically draining game. He then, for my money, hit his most important cross ever. I, like many thousands of others, was locked out of the ground that night, so I didn't see Ray Kennedy's headed goal live, but it's still one of my all-time favourite Arsenal goals, even in grainy black and white.

Santi Cazorla is the only Arsenal player I've ever seen who is able to play as assuredly with either foot as the unassuming 'Geordie' Armstrong did in his heyday. There were, perhaps, better technical players in our first Double-winning team, but none with the heart, soul, drive and dynamism of the greatest Englishman never to represent his country as a full international. He was the engine room of the team in his day, because despite the fact that he was a nominal winger, more usually on the left, his energy simply overflowed everywhere on the pitch, wherever it was required, and I've never seen a harder working Arsenal man in our club's shirt.

You can't mention Geordie and not talk of his part in a Double winning side, a side that included quality aerial targets as Radford and Kennedy for him to target his crosses at. George could provide the pin-point delivery from either flank – not just on the run, but also with in-swinging and out-swinging corners – with either foot and from either side of the pitch. His astounding stamina enabled him to tackle back almost without stopping – but there was far more to Geordie than his pre-emptive impersonation of the Duracell Bunny.

Perhaps it was the arrival of Peter Marinello that spurred him on, or maybe the coming together of a great Arsenal team with the added incentive of having a couple of great target men to find, either way, it was once estimated that he had a hand in more than half our team's goals during 1970/71 Double season.

My favourite Armstrong goals are the pair he scored against Spurs in a 2-0 win in 1970, although none were better than his 30-yarder against Manchester United in 1965. Wingers were out of favour during Alf Ramsey's England reign, which is a great shame, otherwise Geordie would surely have earned some well-deserved international caps. He certainly had as much ability as any of the other England wide men of his era and, in my view, way more than most.

Since his time at Arsenal I feel we've been fortunate enough to have enjoyed so many truly world class players, that I cannot include Geordie in my all-time best Arsenal XI these days, but whenever I pick a *favourite* Arsenal XI, his will always be one of the first names on the team sheet. It was a real privilege to watch him play and I even got to tell him that when I all but bumped into him at an FA Cup Semi Final at Villa Park – a time when he was coaching with the Arsenal and he really was under no obligation to stop and chat with a fan. But stop he did and a more pleasant, modest, unassuming and gracious individual it would be difficult to imagine. They do say you should beware meeting your heroes, but that just wasn't the case with George Armstrong.

Brian Dawes – Arsenal fan

One of the great pleasures of football fandom is the memory of past heroes and reflections on their impact, not only on one's own life, but also on those of the thousands of fellow admirers. Memories, of course, are a personal matter and can obviously be good, bad or indifferent, but they are there and sometimes transfer from the subconscious to the conscious at odd times.

The other day I was engaged in attempting to insulate my loft, but in moving the contents I'd stored there, I came across an old suitcase, which I knew contained all my Arsenal memorabilia. Now, I'm useless at DIY, but I am very good at reminiscing and 'living in the past.' I first attended a match at Highbury in 1962, and still recall that wonderful first-ever view of the pitch and the excitement of being in the crowd. We were fairly poor during most of the Sixties, but perhaps my other great passion, following rock music, made up for it and, as my love of the Kinks, for example, grew, so did my awareness of a player who I can't recall seeing play a bad game, a player who had a tremendous influence in his lengthy time at Arsenal.

I went to a rugby-playing school but, most Saturday morning matches gave us enough time to catch the 84 bus to Arnos Grove from St Albans, then catch the tube to Arsenal. Gradually, I went to more and more matches, including away ones, and took a great interest in the performances of Arsenal's left winger, George Armstrong, as the team began to improve, and eventually, in the early Seventies, gave us such pleasure as cups and titles were won. Nowadays, of course, we have named shirts, give ourselves Arsenal-related Twitter names and other social media methods of displaying our allegiance, but my distraction from insulating showed me that, back then, we wrote the names of players and rock bands on our school exercise books! It seemed all my books had at least one 'George Armstrong' on the cover, but my maths book was adorned with: 'Geordie, Geordie Armstrong, Geordie Armstrong on the wing...' Heaven knows what my teachers thought, especially as underneath was written 'Hendrix' and in different colours 'Pink Floyd'.

On reflection, the period from 1968 'til 1974 was my favourite Arsenal time as Geordie became a mainstay of the team and 'the best player never to play for England' as we said at the time. Of course Radford, McLintock, Graham, Kennedy, George are names etched into all vintage Gooners' memories, but I always loved Geordie's play which, to me, was so good that a quality performance was a 'given' in each game.

Every game I saw him play provided cameos of excellence, brilliance, artistry and graft – how his teammates and the managers must have loved him. I recall visions of a darting, scuttling run with the ball, pin-point crosses and set pieces – plus tireless commitment to both defence and attack. Curiously I don't actually recall a goal of his, but, as I read the programmes contained in my suitcase, vivid memories flashed back of Geordie in action, accompanied by a lexicon of adjectives such as 'neat', 'tidy', 'accurate', 'skilful', 'industrious', 'fast', 'precise' and 'brave'.

Later, during my lengthy career as a PE teacher, many of those Geordie Armstrong descriptors featured on the reports of unknowing pupils – I thank you George for the subconscious vocabulary you instilled. 'How are you getting on?' came a shout from below the loft...'oh, ummm, not too bad....' Shaken out of my reverie I focused on my top three memories of George, before returning to the mundane reality of the loft.

It's a tense and potentially heart breaking day as Arsenal take on Stoke in the 1971 FA Cup Semi Final at Hillsborough against Stoke. From 0-2 a goal is scored to give us hope and Arsenal pile on the pressure in the last minute and win a corner. It's taken from the right of the goal by Geordie and as usual it is pinpoint and invites five, yes five Arsenal players to head it in to equalise... saved on the line by a hand... and Storey puts away the penalty.

It's the league decider at White Hart Lane May 3, 1971, we are a couple of minutes from achieving the 0-0 draw we need to secure the title, with 1-0 being the only other score that would do. I'm in the Park Lane End, just to the right of the goal, not a Spurs fan in sight as Geordie hugs the touchline, dribbles to the byline and crosses a perfect accurate out-swinger to the edge of the six-yard box and Ray Kennedy buries it!

I am at Wembley on May 8, 1971 – Arsenal are bossing the game and will surely score soon... the ball is crossed into the box and a perfectly timed late run by Geordie produces a bullet header from six-yards, but Clemence makes a fantastic save – perhaps that was our chance gone!?

Many footballers' abilities are subject to hyperbole but, based on a long time playing, watching, studying and coaching sport, for me, the mark of greatness is the ability to deliver what is needed, when it was needed, under the severest pressure. Geordie Armstrong was able to do this and that to me is a great player.

Ian Minto – Arsenal fan

If I had to go through the best Arsenal teams of the past, Geordie Armstrong is one of the first names I would write down. Why? Because he stood out as, I'll put it very simply, a bloody good player. He wasn't flamboyant, never set the pitch on fire but was bloody good, consistently working hard for the team every game. He was an Arsenal man through and through and, in my teens, he seemed to be an ever present in the side, the player who you knew would be on that team sheet and we were always grateful for it.

I can remember him playing on both wings and was equally good on either side; I never quite decided which foot was his strongest, much like I cannot with Cazorla today. For some reason today's players struggle with crosses, but Geordie always delivered with a quality and accuracy that was astounding considering it was normally at the end of long run up the wing. And who can forget 1971 with Armstrong crossing the ball to Ray Kennedy against Tottenham for the League title.

My favourite memory is mentioned above, but I have to recall an incident that always brings a smile to my face. It involves the protection he received from the team. I can't remember the club we played, but I was in the North Bank when Geordie cut in from the left wing and was about to pass to Radford, who was completely in the clear, when suddenly, he was hit from behind and fell to the ground. In those days, of course, it was because someone had made 'real' contact. How could they do this to poor Geordie?

The crowd were incensed. A foul was awarded and, following treatment, he and the game continued. Within a couple of minutes the 'perpetrator' of the foul received the ball and a noise rose from the crowd, a bit like a moan that got louder and louder, before I realised the cause. There, accelerating away from the Clock End, was Peter Storey... Everyone in the ground knew what was going to happen.

And it did. Storey struck at such a speed that the opponent flew into the air with an ear-splitting scream. The funniest thing was, the ref did nothing and Storey walked away as if nothing had happened – giving a sly wink in the direction of Geordie. It was a brilliant moment and I laughed all the way home.

Pat Whelton – Arsenal fan

Following Arsenal, for me at least, has nothing to do with winning trophies etc – although, of course, it's great to win those too. In my view, Arsenal is a 'way of life', one which involves having an affection and deep love of the club.

Many times over the years I have asked myself why players don't have that same feeling, however there are exceptions. One that immediately springs to my mind is George Armstrong. In my day, fans loved a player that gave 'his all' in every game – that is why George was loved by so many – because he showed courage and commitment in abundance.

I was a fan of Arsenal throughout George's illustrious career at the club, which included playing in every game during the Double winning season of 1971. One has to remember that George played against some of the toughest defenders in the World then – Ron Harris, Tommy Smith, Johnny Giles, Norman Hunter, Alan Mullery etc. – the kind of players who took no prisoners, so for George to be ever present was a testament to his courage.

Geordie didn't score that many goals during his time with Arsenal but he laid on so many for others. One I will never ever forget is the way he set Ray Kennedy up to head in the winner at White Hart Lane to win Arsenal the first League title in 18 years. He bust a gut to stop the ball going out of play before crossing for Ray. Typical of George!

His 'assists' record must be well up there with the best and his passing accuracy, crosses into box, successful tackles made and distance covered during a game would be extremely high too. And how about yellow and red cards? Never, not our Geordie, which is remarkable considering the provocation he faced.

I travelled to many away game during that time and he was highly respected by all fans. Sometimes groups of supporters would gather outside the main entrance of away grounds to greet the players when they arrived and without fail, George always stopped to acknowledged us and came over to sign autographs with a smile and for a friendly chat. George respected us fans too which, sadly, is rare quality in a player in my opinion. You somehow felt as though he was one of us, which, of course, he was!

George would swap from right to left to cause confusion in opponents' defence and was often seen making last ditch tackles in our own penalty area. Geordie was a true team player, in the real sense of the word. I have so many fond memories and always enjoyed joining in with the singing of 'Geordie, Geordie Armstrong on the wing!!' Many players are wrongly called legends, but George Armstrong really is a true legend at Arsenal. Thanks for the memories.

Peter Nelson – Arsenal fan

I became Arsenal crazy in 1968 as a seven-year-old boy, as obsessed as my dad, and his dad. We all used to stand in the Clock End, right down by the front barrier, with me holding on to my dad. I truly loved the Arsenal.

At school we played football every time we got a chance and pretending to be our favourite footballer was part of our game. I always had to be George Armstrong, else I would go off in a strop and not play. I even left my hair to grow past my ears, so I could be just like George. He was my idol. Pretending to be him made me feel amazing and I believed, for that instance,

I could play like him. I would run down the wing and cross the ball just like my hero.

On match days we used to get to Highbury extra-early, about an hour and half before kick-off and recall hearing all the players warming up ahead of the game on the training pitch that was behind the clock end. Then, at three o'clock, it was kick-off... "Georgie, Georgie Armstrong, Georgie, Georgie Armstrong". There he was on the wing and we would all watch him charging down the wing. He was so quick, give-and-go, nutmeg, right to the by-line, cross the ball right on to Radford or Kennedy's head, who ever was there first, smash-and-grab. George was the provider. Just before the end of the game my dad would position us so, when the final whistle went, we could jump over the railings and get onto the pitch. First Bob Wilson, "well played Bob", he would pat me on the head... then straight to George, "well played George", he would say "thank you son". What more could I ask for? I would go home singing, "Georgie, Georgie Armstrong, Georgie Armstrong on the wing." He is my hero still to this day.

Brian Lewis – Arsenal fan

I emigrated to Canada in 1966 but, until then, I never missed a home game and the very mention of George Armstrong brings a smile to my face. Standing behind the goal on Highbury's North Bank, watching George bear down on goal from the wing, and hearing the crowd roar their encouragement, will forever remain in my memory.

He was a fan favourite who was not only gifted, but gave everything for his team. In those days fans, above all else, appreciated total commitment and dedication. George Armstrong had both in abundance

I missed a lot of his games after 1966 because football in Canada was not regularly televised, but I followed every newspaper and magazine article and, as such, was fully aware of George's ongoing contribution.

Unique is an interesting word, it means like no other. In my opinion George Armstrong fits into that category.

Peter Skelton – Arsenal fan

My dad and elder brothers would attend Highbury every other weekend to watch the Arsenal. It had been a while (1953) since Arsenal had won anything and real heroes were short on the ground.

By 1965 a young lad by the name of George Armstrong, 'Geordie' to the Arsenal faithful, had started to become a regular in the side. Geordie played on the wing and the crowd would sing "send Georgie down the wing, for one more goal..." For me though, George Armstrong had everything you could want in a footballer. Honesty, he gave everything, skipped over tackles, scored goals, set up goals and worked hard for the team. The Highbury crowd loved him.

Being young myself back then, Geordie excited me. Seeing him run down the wing, take players on and cause all sorts of trouble for defenders was just what this young lad wanted to see. During my early years watching Arsenal, Geordie hardly missed a game and, if I tell you tackles flew in, it would be an understatement – in those days there were much harder players then than you see today. Yet George took all that was thrown at him and came back for more.

After six years of Arsenal going nowhere, Bertie Mee came along. Finally Geordie might get something for his efforts. Firstly reaching two League Cup finals, although sadly ending on the losing side in both, but then onto true success. Geordie helped follow those defeats with an Inter Cities Fairs Cup win in 1970, then helped Arsenal to the Double in 1971. For me, George was a players' player, a gentleman who would never let his team down. Even at a young age I could never understand how George never got to be capped by England. So it was fitting that George would become (for a time) the leading Arsenal appearance holder.

In those early days I had other heroes too – namely John Radford and Ray Kennedy – but Geordie was the player that got me excited while I stood on the famous terraces come rain or shine. Geordie is why I also played on the wing as a lad and stayed there during my teens and twenties, until age and injury took their toll.

A fabulous, much underrated footballer and the reason why, over the years since, I've appreciated other craftsmen such as Rix, Rocastle, Limpar, Overmars and Pires – I love seeing wide players take on defenders – something that was instilled in me by Geordie Armstrong, a true Arsenal legend, who was sadly taken from us in 2000. George was certainly taken too early, but at least he was doing what he loved, working with the team he loved. RIP George Armstrong, you will never be forgotten.

Steve Martin – Arsenal fan

My memories of Geordie Armstrong, the player, are of a man who never stopped running. He was absolutely everywhere, had unbelievable stamina, was so consistent and was hardly ever injured. During the Double season he played all 42 League games and was the main provider for Radford and Kennedy, with his gift for providing deadly, pin-point crosses with either foot and with amazing regularity.

I was fortunate enough to see him play in every home game that season, as well as the title decider at White Hart Lane, where Geordie provided the cross for Ray Kennedy to score the winner – I was also there for the FA Cup Final at Wembley

I met him once, in the 1990s, outside Highbury midweek with my son Neil. There wasn't a game on, so there weren't many people about, but there was Geordie, one of my heroes, walking down Avenell Road. I asked him if he minded signing his autograph for me and he duly obliged. All he wanted to talk about was how well The Arsenal had played the previous Saturday. It was just like talking with another fan, he was so down to earth. You could tell he loved Arsenal Football Club and cared deeply from the way he spoke about them.

My brother Tony also met him on the Tube after the 1993 FA Cup Semi-Final, apparently Geordie had missed the team bus! Tony was understandably ecstatic at beating the old enemy and so was Geordie. My brother, slightly inebriated, told him how much he loved him as a player and how he'd modelled his playing style on him before kissing Geordie on the cheek! Geordie was also pleased as punch at beating Spurs and told my brother he couldn't wait to phone Dave Mackay, who he said would be absolutely gutted we had beaten them! Geordie was not only a fantastic Arsenal player, but a great man as well – he always had time for us fans.

Gary Lawrence, Basildon – Arsenal fan

I grew up watching George Armstrong playing in Combination matches, my dad would watch the football from the North Bank, whilst I ran around playing on the terraces. We lived just around the corner from Highbury, so it was prominent to the area I grew up in, and a big part of my early memories. Although we all knew Geordie as a great player – arguably the first Arsenal winger I think of – he was not a regular goalscorer. However, there is no doubt that he set plenty up, including the one that Kennedy scored to win us the title at the Lane. Had it been in this day and age with OPTA stats, I believe he would have had a fantastic record in that department.

I remember us playing Chelsea at Highbury in a Cup replay back in '73 – Geordie had been fouled on the edge of the penalty area up at the Clock End. We were one down at the time and the ref awarded a free kick. For me, it certainly looked like a penalty but the referee had only awarded a free kick on the edge of the area. After what seemed like an eternity, the Arsenal players persuaded Geordie to have a word with his linesman, which he duly did – there was no doubt what the linesman was going to tell the referee after that and he was forced to change his decision. We equalised from the spot kick, then went on to win the game.

A quick YouTube search is always good for jolting my memory and, after typing in 'George Armstrong', and coming up with General Custer and someone who had played ice hockey for the Toronto Maple Leafs, I clicked the link to a game against Derby at Highbury that George had played in. The piece at the end of the *Big Match* highlights shows George being interviewed by

Brian Moore who introduces the piece by saying that Armstrong had been the unanimous choice by the other players to go on the programme and be their guest, which demonstrates what a popular person he was at the club... liked by players and fans alike. We can all pick our favourites but Geordie was part of the very fabric of the club and I can't think of my time growing up without thinking of George in some capacity.

Jeff Stevens – Arsenal fan

I first started going to Highbury in 1971/72, unable to keep the smile from my ten-year-old face through sheer excitement, having to pinch myself as the team ran onto the pitch lead by Frank Mclintock. Red and white in the flesh, wow! I still recall that nerves butterfly feeling and the players' names that left such lasting memories. They were such fabulous times, especially under the floodlights with the added worry of having to get up for school the next day. One thing that always stays with me is Geordie, sleeves hanging, legs like pistons always giving 100%, everything good in the game going through him. So many great names have worn the Arsenal shirt, but that little fella made it all tick. He seemed to be everywhere, both flanks, crosses galore for Radford, Kennedy and George, I still love them all, but Geordie was just that bit more special. Thank you George, you made sure the Arsenal bug in me was there to stay – a true gentleman of the game and a real influence on this Gunner.

David Greenberg – Arsenal fan

If ever there was a football player who deserved plaudits, it would be Geordie Armstrong – he made the hairs stand up on the back of my neck time and time again. I even got to run around the hallowed turf of Highbury with him on that famous April night in 1970. He was a proper footballer, no fuss, but all heart. He was a hero to me as 14-year-old girl – I thought he ran like the wind. That's my lasting memory of him and it will remain so forever.

Madge Bassett – Arsenal fan

He was simply the kind of player that made the hairs on the back of your neck stand on end whenever he came on to the pitch. As a man, he may have been small in stature, but he was a giant of football. He could run forever, and in all my 56 years of watching football, I have never seen a player with a better work ethic both charging forward and bustling back to help defend. He was instrumental in ending Arsenal's dismal run of 17 years without a trophy when he was outstanding in the 3-0 win over Anderlecht, which, to this day, is my best ever experience at a match – even surpassing Anfield in 1989. He was a vital player in the Double year; setting up Kennedy to score the winner against Spurs which on its own secured legend status. My memories of Geordie will go with me to my grave, and it brings a tear to my eye just writing about him. Taken from us too early, God bless you Geordie – you certainly blessed Arsenal.

Steve Cooper – Secretary, Arsenal Supporter's Trust

The term 'unsung hero' was coined with George Armstrong in mind I'm sure, as it sums him up completely. Hard working, honest, fair. They are just a few of the ways you could describe the diminutive character that so characterised The Arsenal of 1969-1972.

He would work tirelessly through games, while others would put in half the shift he did and took all the plaudits. The best analogy I can come up with to describe Geordie is this: If Radford, George, Kennedy, Wilson etc were the goodies inside the can, then George Armstrong was the can opener. He was the one who made all things possible for those players, with his behind the scenes industriousness. George Armstrong was everything a sportsman worthy of the title should be. He was Arsenal to the core and is held in such high esteem by all those lucky enough to have seen him play – his reputation goes before him. George Armstrong was a footballer and a gentleman but, above all, an 'Arsenal Man' to the end.

Des Powell – Arsenal fan

I really loved him as a player as he gave 100% every game. He was a small footballer, but in my view, was the unsung hero of the Double winning side. He had two great feet and would play down the left or right equally as effectively and often switch flanks in the same game.

He had an engine that kept going for the full 90 minutes and I remember him running non-stop, I recall him being able to deliver a ball onto a sixpence from either side and with both feet; he really was a true Arsenal great. I know people will say to me, you only look back and remember the good times, but I cannot honestly remember him having a bad day at the office. The team often did, but not Geordie.

In those days the thick leather boots soaked up the rain so, the longer you played, the heavier your boots got. The old Highbury pitch was a bog in the winter, as were most pitches, there was no snooker table grass to play on. Today, it would sometimes appear that if anyone plays for Arsenal for more than two years they get called a legend, which of course is rubbish, but Geordie Armstrong was a true Arsenal legend. Of that there is no doubt.

Mick Wilkinson – Arsenal fan

Georgie Armstrong, as I always refer to him, to supporters of a 'reasonable age' will conjure great nostalgia and special memories. It certainly does with me. I was indoctrinated into The Arsenal thanks to another George; my Uncle George. In the late Sixties he used to come to our house in North West London before and after games.

It wasn't the most positive of starts to my Arsenal career really, as my first memories were of leaving for Wembley full of hope and returning very glum after seeing us lose two years running in the League Cup Final; to Leeds United in '68 and, ugh, Swindon Town in '69. My first hero was John Radford, he was, after all, the big number nine centre-forward and, equally importantly to me at the time, shared the same birthday as me; February 22nd.

But the player I most admired, amongst all of Arsenal's quality of that era, as well as pretending to be when I played football myself, was Georgie Armstrong. I'm not going to go into stats about appearances and goals; I'll leave that to others, but I do want to say what he meant to me and what I saw.

It was a different era, no question, a time when squads were small, wages were 'reasonable', transfer fees hadn't gone bananas and teams could win stuff with spirit and teamwork rather than massive investment.

Georgie played left wing and wore the number seven shirt, as did I for the local cubs' team, as all left wingers did in those days; that was the rule! At that was the number that my mum had proudly sewn onto the back of my first Arsenal shirt – Georgie's number seven. I still have a picture of me in that shirt to this day.

He was, and will always remain, an authentic legend and a perfect role model. Georgie was a genuine and honest player, who always gave his all; full of heart and passion. If ever the phrase 'Arsenal through and through' was tailor made for anyone it was for him. George was a terrier with a superlative engine, a non-stop dynamo and a magnificent crosser of a ball. As my Uncle George always said he was, "Either down one end crossing them in or down the other heading them off the line."

Bless you and thank you, George. It was a pleasure and a privilege to see you play so often. With 11 of you in the side we would have been the first Invincibles back then!

Andrew Heasman – Arsenal fan

It was an eight-year-old boy's first visit to Highbury in 1971. The excitement and the memories are with me to this day. West Stand Upper and the walk - up and up the steps - seemingly forever. Then dad and I were there, looking for our entrance as we walked the concourse. Once found, up a few more steps then... the vision of the baize-like green of the pitch, amazing. The smell - cigar smoke! The players emerged. Wow! Arsenal won three-nil that afternoon when a little winger popped on BOTH wings providing pin-

The North Bank's hero

point crosses. I knew little of football's ways then, but that impressed me so much. "Go Geordie" the old men around me cried. This was confusing as I was young, but already knew that George wasn't a Scot! John Radford scored twice that day. Probably from assists from George, memory fails me on that. He was a always a constant fixture in the team as I grew up, even as the team faded. Legend is an overused word in football but George certainly is an Arsenal one. And as I write this, 42 years later, I now know why he was known as "Geordie", but I always smile when I hear his name. What a player!
Chris Ferguson– Arsenal fan

I first saw George Armstrong on November 22, 1969. If I'm honest I don't remember very much as I was only six. It was a cold day, but also more of a passive experience than a fever pitch moment – even though I was sitting in the unreserved seats in the Lower West Stand. If truth be known, I had more than a soft spot for Leeds United at that time. Memories of my first visit to Highbury are few. I remember Terry Neill scoring a penalty in a 1-1 draw.

I was lucky enough to be at Wembley in 1971 and I remember Geordie coming awfully close to scoring. But much of what I've come to know about his early years I've learnt from YouTube and scouring stats books. The George Armstrong I remember bridged two generations of players.

As the Double side faded the next generation of exciting talent – Rix, Brady, Stapleton and O'Leary – took over. Arsenal came pretty close to relegation in the mid-70s and but for tenacious performances from the likes of Geordie, Peter Storey and Alan Ball, it may have happened. They were players from a tough era and wonderful professionals all of them.

What I've come to realise is just what a good player he was. He was quick, gutsy but, more importantly, incredibly two-footed – and boy could he cross a ball – with Radford, Graham and Kennedy supreme in the air. The only other Arsenal player I can compare Geordie to would be Brian Marwood, who did a similar job from the wings in 1988/89 – but Geordie was the far superior player of the two – operating from both wings and far more two-footed.

Geordie chipped in with goals throughout his career at Arsenal and was a virtual ever-present until his departure in 1977. I remember him stealing in at the North Bank end to score the only goal against Liverpool on a cold grey afternoon in 1976. I don't think I can ever remember him complaining or being booked – he just got on with his job with the minimum of fuss. I am sure that was why he was one of the first names on the team sheet for many, many years. George Armstrong will always be one of my favourite players – what a wonderful footballer.
Andrew Tilley – Arsenal fan

I would like to thank all of the above for their fabulous and generous words and memories. I have met and spoken to so many who have played and worked with Geordie that the warmth and love felt for him no longer surprises me. It is wonderful, however, that the memories seem so vivid and the admiration for Geordie, and what he meant to those cheering him on from the stands and terraces, remains so strong to this day.

Arsenal have had many great sides since the all-conquering 1970/71 team, to which Geordie was so integral, but to some supporters it seems, in their hearts, it will always be 'Geordie Armstrong on the wing!' I will end this chapter with one more contribution, from a fan who actually never saw Geordie play a competitive match for Arsenal.

I saw Geordie play just the once, in Michael Watson's testimonial, 13 years after he retired, it was March 1993. He had more energy and skill than many wingers who are playing today, with Liam Brady spraying some beautiful passes out to him. Seriously, he had white hair, and it was surreal watching him sprinting with such energy and real pace. It was an amazing sight. It is just such a shame that's my only live memory of the great man.

Marios Ioannou – Arsenal fan

A MENTOR IN TRANSITION: 1973 TO 1977

I was interested to get some feedback from the mid-Seventies era, when the new generation of young stars mentioned earlier, were pushing through. Soon after the triumphs and highs of the 1969-72 period, Arsenal found themselves a side in transition – some of the legends were sold by Mee, or fell out with him, but Armstrong remained a constant in the team week in week out through a more troubled time, a period in which Geordie, Rice, Radford, Simpson and Kelly provided experience and guidance to a new group of young charges, led by the most prodigious of them all, Liam Brady.

Brady arrived aged just 15, in the summer after the Double season. The 1971/72 side was still extremely competitive, but in December '71 the club bought Alan Ball, which Brady reflects was a signing that created problems within the club. Frictions were created apparently as he came for big money, reputedly on much higher wages than any of the Double winning side. This friction was felt particularly with the younger element of the Double side, such as Charlie George, Eddie Kelly and Ray Kennedy – and so a golden era came to an abrupt end.

Bertie Mee seemed to lose the grip of the situation and the loss of Don Howe at the end of 1971 had not helped. Burtenshaw had taken over, but moved on after two seasons, and it was Bobby Campbell who arrived and encouraged Mee to go with the kids. Bobby was popular with Geordie and Alan Ball, but the old side was breaking up.

Liam got to know George as a young player and lived near him in Winchmore Hill. George would often take Liam into training. "He always had big cars and I always knew the music would be on a loud as could be. He liked speed and always drove too fast.

To a young player he could have appeared like a flash superstar, but Geordie was not like the others. He was totally a family man, and when the other married guys would stay out drinking, Geordie would always have one, then get home to Marj and the kids, and he'd always insisting on buying the first round at the bar."

"Geordie used to always ask the younger players, particularly Wilf Rostron and me, if they were okay for money. He was ridiculously generous and he would ask the young lads to baby sit and pay them silly money, giving them £20 each when going rate would be a fiver. He had sorted Wilf and me out with our lodgings where he had lodged as a younger pro and, when he popped round some evenings, he would barely be through the door and he would say "Come on lads get the crib board out." The three of us would play cards while Marj would chat to the landlady, Mrs Cranston, whilst the kids would play and have cake." He was clearly not only a great role model, but a mentor and a friend too.

Brady said Geordie was super fit and could run all day, whilst he himself was not blessed with the same appetite, Geordie had it by the bucket-load. Rumour had it that after a hard day's pre-season everyone else would be tired and relaxing, but Geordie would still be out running. "Bally once came in to training saying he had seen Geordie outside building a wall after a hard day of pre-season, when everyone else would have been home on the couch."

Brady recalls that he led by example and by encouragement; "He was always keen to help and guide with great patience. He was genuinely pleased when I did well and, even when I was playing on left ahead of Geordie, he would only praise me. Geordie would take his anger out on those who had left him out, not those who had taken his place."

Ultimately, of course, Brady played many games with Geordie, including the testimonial against Barcelona, which he describes as; "a great night for George with 36,000 at Highbury. You would never normally get such a big crowd for a testimonial, but that proved he was such a popular player."

Brady confirmed, as one would suspect, that Geordie was popular with all the young guys coming through. Perhaps it was, in part, because when Armstrong was asked to play for the reserves he would always help the young players. "Others were not like that. Geordie simply did not know how to play without giving 100%. Whereas some others I could mention had an attitude that was more 'what the fuck am I doing here'?"

"Geordie always had a scheme going on in his mind. He was a bit of a 'Del Boy'... Not in a wheeler-dealer way, but in the dreamer sense that said 'I am going to get lucky one day'. He also ran the lottery consortium at the club." And then, with a wry smile, Brady concluded; "What must be said is that Geordie loved life!"

"Everybody loved Geordie, all through the years. His team mates in the Sixties and Seventies, all us kids growing up who eventually became first team players, we all loved him and then the generation of players he coached, they all loved him too."

FRANK STAPLETON – ARSENAL 1974–1981

It was patently obvious that Brady had a close bond with Armstrong, but what about his fellow countryman who, by 1975, was the one on the end of the master's crosses?

Frank Stapleton, having left Arsenal 19 years before Geordie's passing, ensured he was at the funeral, such was the impact of the man on his fledgling career in North London. "For the youngsters at that time in the early Seventies, Geordie was always approachable, always funny and a man you felt you could go to with your footballing problems. He was so down to Earth and unaffected by his stature in the game. To describe his as a modest man would be an understatement."

"As a youngster we used to train on separate pitches to the first team and would not necessarily mix with the star players – we'd only ever go through the first team dressing room to get to the boot room, for boot cleaning duties." That situation is a far cry from today of course but, for Stapleton, it taught him respect. "However, whilst most of the first-teamers might not know you, or take little interest in you, Geordie was different. For Geordie it did not matter who you were and, after one or two meetings, you felt warm in his presence and felt like you knew him." Stapleton muses that "Perhaps some youngsters felt threatened by the first-teamers, but not Geordie, he had such an endearing way about him that people just wanted to be in his company, and were relaxed in it."

When he was breaking into the side with Brady it was a difficult time for the Arsenal, near the lower end of Division One, but George Armstrong carried the team with his constant positivity and encouragement. Arsenal beat the drop by just six points, which was a little too close for comfort considering the recent achievements at the club. Geordie had been virtually ever-present from December onwards, which had proved critical.

Stapleton was, of course, the centre-forward tasked to get on the end of the Armstrong crosses and knew whether his run was near post or far, so the magician would pick him out. "I never played with, or saw, another player that could pick a player out, and cross on the run, like Geordie could. His accuracy was legendary. "

Stapleton admits being confused as to why Terry Neill sold Geordie, when he seemingly still had so much to offer; "He could still supply cross after cross, he was never injured and had the fitness of a player five years his junior. Geordie was not rewarded for his loyalty."

Like Brady, he remembers being petrified by Geordie's driving and, on one occasion, when they were both injured, Armstrong offered him a lift back to North London from Colney. He was driving an automatic red Mini at the time; "I had never been in an automatic car before and Geordie was flying in and out of traffic with his music blaring out."

"There is no doubt that Geordie liked his music loud, Motown, Rock or Classical he had varied tastes, but he had a thing for the Beatles or John Lennon in particular. Every time Lennon was on the TV Geordie would come into training the next day going on about Yoko Ono. It became a running joke as he would always say in his broad accent, 'What the fucking hell is John Lennon doing with that fucking ugly Yoko Ono?'"

WILF ROSTRON – ARSENAL 1973-77

Part of the same youth, then reserve team as both Brady and Stapleton, and as we heard, Liam's co-lodger, was Wilf Rostron, a player who, ironically, was perhaps being readied to finally replace Geordie on the left wing at Arsenal. That situation never emerged though, as both were to leave Arsenal in 1977. Rostron was sold to Sunderland before enjoying a fabulous 300-plus game career at Watford, where he was part of the Hornet's best ever side during an impressive decade. And, just like Stapleton, Wilf remembers Geordie with huge affection. "He was a great ambassador for the North East. No nonsense, down to earth, a real 'get on with it' bloke."

"From the age of 17 I got to know Geordie and he lived his life like he played his football – he just continuously did the right thing, with no confusion, no over elaboration, just to the point, effective for the good of his team, both on the pitch and those around him in life. Week in, week out, he just tried to do the right things."

In asking Rostron 'what had he learned from the master', it was fascinating to watch him pause, think, then laugh as he did so before saying; "I always used to dribble with the ball too long and perhaps try to beat an extra man, or the same man twice, before crossing. I thought I was clever with all kinds of trickery until, one day, when playing for the reserves, I was taught a stark lesson." The centre forward that day was none other than John Radford who was getting tired of young Wilf's over elaboration. He was continually making his runs into the box only for the cross not to arrive as Rostron tried to beat another or get to the bye-line for the perfect ball. "You see, Radford was used to the Armstrong service and the cross being delivered early. Radford's advice to me was strong and to the point and he boomed 'Will you stop dilly-dallying out there and just get the cross in at the first opportunity like Geordie does!'"

Rostron carried that lesson with him throughout his career and, even today, when he watches players try and beat a man before getting a cross in, he thinks; "Why do that when there is no need, Geordie Armstrong would not have done."

Rostron questions whether Armstrong was appreciated as much outside of Arsenal as he was by his own fans and team mates, with other players perhaps demanding more media attention; "but the final analysis is all about end product and, with Geordie, that was a constant supply of quality crosses delivered at the right time. I can't imagine a single person saying a bad word about him, which is unusual in football."

BRENDAN BATSON, MBE – ARSENAL 1971-74

Before adopting a prominent role at the PFA, Batson was one of the pioneering young, black footballers in England, indeed, he was Arsenal's first black first-teamer. Like the Armstrongs, Batson also lost some one dear to him, his wife of 38 years, Cecily, passed away in 2009 – she was just 57, one year older than Geordie when he died.

Batson has fond memories of his limited time with Geordie, the three years that came after the famous League and Cup Double, and recalls complete and utter warmth and openness from the Arsenal great. He is not being critical of his senior Arsenal team mates, because it would have been the same at all clubs back then, but most players had little time for the youngsters. However, with Bob Wilson, and particularly George Armstrong, it was different. "He was one of those who really made you feel at ease in his company and he was very generous with his advice." For Batson, a budding right-back, Geordie's time and guidance were invaluable. "He would give the youngster tips and pointers on how to play against wingers, which, given that Geordie was the best winger in the League, was priceless. I remember, even when Don Howe was working with me and Peter Marinello on wing and full-back play ahead of a reserves game, Geordie would come over and take time out to assist."

"The 1971 side was full of tremendous professionals to admire and respect. They were great to watch at work, and to learn from, but it was Geordie who left the lasting impression on me. I valued the advice and support Geordie gave when I left Arsenal, which I have no doubt helped me succeed at West Brom."

He was also not at all surprised with Armstrong's post-playing success when he returned to the club; "He had a great connection with the young players at Arsenal, so it was no surprise to me that he went on after his playing days to become such a superb coach of younger players."

RICHIE POWLING – ARSENAL 1973-81

For those of us following Arsenal in the early Seventies, Richie Powling was earmarked to be a major star, destined to dominate the heart of defence for years to come. There is little doubt that he was a highly talented centre-back, one who made his debut in 1973, ironically, against a Queens Park Rangers side marshalled by the very player he was hoping to emulate – a certain Frank McLintock.

Richie had been a regular in the reserves from the age of only 15 and, on the cusp of his 17th birthday, was delighted to be taken away on the end of season first-team tour to Canada. He played twice alongside Peter Simpson, but the nervous teenager clearly remembers the man who was on hand to calm his trepidation. "Geordie Armstrong made a point of speaking to me every morning on tour, "All okay Richie?" he would says, "Are they looking after you? If you need anything at all, or just want to talk, you know where to come." He was fantastic. There were others on the tour that looked out for me, but none more so than Geordie – that applied on the pitch too. He was a true gentleman of football."

"As I played more regularly for the first team during 1974 and 1975, Geordie remained a constant mentor and inspiration during games. He was so fit that he would make a point of running all the way back from the wing to encourage me if I made a mistake"

He describes him as "genuinely caring" and the trait of continually running back to reassure him or encourage him as "virtually unique". "George was an inspiration for all young players because of his incredible enthusiasm and unfailing commitment to the team, whatever the circumstances. He was also immensely fit with a heart as big as a lion!" What a perfect description.

Powling continued; "At any level of football, supporters will always love the players who give the most on the pitch and those who show loyalty to their club. Hence Geordie was the most loved of players at the Arsenal and rightly so."

Powling was a first team regular with Geordie in 1975/76, but dreadful ankle and knee injuries curtailed and, ultimately, ended a promising career in professional football. The disappointment of having everything taken from him meant that he did not watch any football, live or on television, for about six years. He simply could not bear to watch those he should have been competing with, playing the game he loved so much. When Richie did return, as a coach in non-League football, he was not surprised to see his mentor earning a growing reputation as a top coach.

"He always knew how to encourage and illicit the best from his colleagues and I always expected him to coach when he concluded his playing career. Geordie seemed to intuitively know the right thing to say, and when you are coaching players, that is an invaluable asset. That, of course, combined with a deep love for and knowledge of the game."

Even as the reserve team boss at Arsenal in the 1990s, Armstrong continued to assist his former team mate, twice taking Arsenal sides down to play Powling's Sudbury Town in pre-season matches and, on one occasion, a side that included ten internationals in the staring eleven; "That simply had to be Geordie's doing..." Powling insists.

GRAHAM RIX – ARSENAL 1975-88

It is fitting that we bring this chapter to a close by talking to the man who, ultimately, was to fill Geordie Armstrong's significant boots after he left Arsenal – Graham Rix adopting the left of Arsenal's midfield unstintingly for the next decade. Indeed, it seems fitting that eight years after Geordie crossed for Kennedy to win us our first domestic trophy, and the first portion of the Double, it was Rix, from a similar position on the left wing, who crossed for Alan Sunderland, to win the Gunners' next piece of silverware after another long gap.

To Graham Rix, travelling down to from South Yorkshire as a teenager to train at Arsenal in the early 1970s, George Armstrong and the rest of the Double-winners were like Gods, and when he signed as an apprentice in 1974, he could not believe that the likes of Simpson, Storey, Radford, and most particularly Geordie, would take the time to talk to him – but they did. Even now Rix looks back and recalls how lucky he was to be thrown into the reserves at Arsenal so early, and to find himself playing alongside these heroes at only 16 years of age. Some of those players may have been out of the first team at that late stage, either injured or out of favour perhaps, but

according to Rix, they all played at their optimum and all gave their time and experience to help the youngsters – but none more so than Geordie.

"Geordie would turn up in the morning looking grumpy and mumbling to himself, but it only took and kind word or a 'Good morning Geordie' and his face would transform. With Geordie, a smile was always only a second away."

For Rix, forging his way into the first team picture at Highbury, there was much to admire about Armstrong, but despite his easy going nature, there was no doubt in his mind at any stage, that Geordie was a 100% winner. "Whether it was in a training game, a hand of cards, a snooker outing to Southgate, or on a Saturday in the first team wearing red and white, Geordie Armstrong played to win."

Rix used to watch the matches with the rest of the youth team every other Saturday at Highbury and understood immediately why the Arsenal fans adored him so much. "He was a whirlwind of a footballer, perpetually in motion, creating the attacks and supporting Sammy Nelson at left-back when the team were defending. He was always one of Arsenal's best performers, even when the team was fairing badly."

Graham Rix made his first team debut towards the end of the 1976/77 season and, in doing so, Geordie was moved to the right flank, before his summer move away from the club. Rix began the following season as first choice on the left wing and that was the end of that for Geordie.

I could see, even then, that Terry Neill found it difficult to manage players he'd played with, and that he wanted to put his own personal stamp on the Arsenal team. I've often been asked about taking Geordie's place, but I felt he still had so much to offer – Geordie, Liam and myself could certainly have played together – in fact Geordie could have even moved inside and easily used his experience as a box-to-box central midfielder."

Later, as a youth coach at Chelsea, Rix recalls meeting up again with Geordie, who was managing the Arsenal reserves. "It seemed so obvious why George Graham had chosen Geordie for that role – he was the perfect fit. I could not think of a better guy to teach young players – not just about how to be a footballers – but how to be an Arsenal footballer."

"Not just anyone could carry off that role at a big club, managing a team of youngsters, all wanting to be first teamer, and more senior players, who don't want to be there, isn't an easy task. However, Geordie was perfect as he could speak to anyone, at any level, and get through to them. Geordie would speak in exactly the same way to the Queen as he would to a man on the street."

Rix went on to explain that whenever the two met each other whilst he was learning the coaching trade at another club, the conversation was never about Geordie, it was always about Rix. "Geordie would ask how I was getting on, whether I had any new coaching techniques, about what I was learning at Chelsea, when it should have been the other way around.

That was the nature of the man, generous, thoughtful and always genuinely pleased to see friends or an ex-colleague doing well."

"He was respected throughout the game – as a player and as a coach. It seemed that everybody in the game knew and loved Geordie and, when he died, it shook me to my bones."

So there we have it, a friend and a mentor to six young professionals, learning their trade in the toughest League and at the finest club. During a difficult era for Arsenal these players admit they owe so much to Geordie Armstrong. Whether the needed advice, guidance, or a just a kind word, he was always on hand and let them know he was there to help them in whatever way he could – whether that meant some tactical wisdom, or an extra twenty quid for a baby-sitting shift! On the pitch, Geordie inspired them: leading by example, both technically and with a never say die attitude which bred a winning mentality at the club.

However, Geordie had not been as happy for a while and had even spoken to Bertie Mee about moving on during the 1975/76 season. Mee had asked him to stay on to the end of the season before the new manager, Terry Neill, an old team mate of Geordie's from the 1960s, asked him to stay until the following Christmas.

In the end Armstrong remained at Arsenal further 12 months, until the end of 1976/77, during which he played 37 of the 42 league games – his last competitive match for Arsenal was a stirring 3-2 defeat at Old Trafford against Manchester United.

Armstrong played in an end of season tour of Norway in May 1977, which, as you will discover, was another ironic coincidence – Geordie would be back in Norway sooner than he probably expected.

In the final game of that trip, against Nessegoten: Rix, Powling, Rostron and Brady all played too. There were to be a few last appearances in July, on a pre-season tour of Australia, but they proved to be the end of the line for Geordie as an Arsenal player – the Armstrong era was over.

IF GEORDIE WAS PLAYING TODAY

Having reached this point of the book, my hope is that you will certainly know Geordie Armstrong fairly well and enjoyed hearing from the players, coaches, journalists and fans who were there when George was at his best. However, as I am still firmly in a reflective mode, I thought it would be a fascinating aside to ask my collaborators and contributors to give Geordie a modern context – by asking them if they could liken Geordie to a player, or players, of a more modern era, along with an estimate of how much a 1971 vintage Armstrong would be worth on the transfer market nowadays. If Arsenal would be fool enough to sell him, obviously. Here's what they said.

Who would I compare to Geordie? I found it very difficult to think of anyone would was so box-to-box in the modern era – perhaps a combination of Andre Kanckelskis and David Beckham? Blimey, that suggests he would be worth an awful lot in today's market!
George Graham – Arsenal 1966-72 & 1986-95

"The first name that springs to mind is Ryan Giggs – for his tireless box-to-box work and excellent crossing – although perhaps I could suggest a combination of Giggs and Pires? Thierry Henry once said he would not have achieved anywhere near as much without Robert Pires and I feel Radford and Kennedy would say the same of Geordie. As for placing a value on Geordie at his peak in today's transfer market, well, the sky's the limit. They threw away the mould when they made Geordie!"
David Dein – Arsenal Vice Chairman 1983-2008

For work-rate and perhaps for being wrongly under-estimated outside of Arsenal, I would compare him to Ray Parlour. However, for crossing accuracy, just think of David Beckham, but with pace! It is so hard to think of a value for Geordie today, but every team in the Premiership would compete for his signature, of that I guarantee."
David Court – Arsenal 1962-70 & 1996-2014

Someone like Ronaldo would still be the exception, but Geordie, for me, would sit in the next bracket. He was the best winger of his generation and would be worth £30 to £40 million today.
Alex Forsyth – Manchester United 1972-78

It is so difficult to compare Geordie to anyone who is playing now, but the player who first came to mind is Frank Ribery.
Liam Brady – Arsenal 1973-1980

There are simply no players today with his pace and speed of thought, and certainly none with his crossing ability. The closest for work rate and intensity would be David Rocastle. He would be worth a minimum of £30 million, but if Draxler is worth £37 million, then Geordie would be worth much more.
Stewart Houston – Arsenal Assistant Manager 1990-96

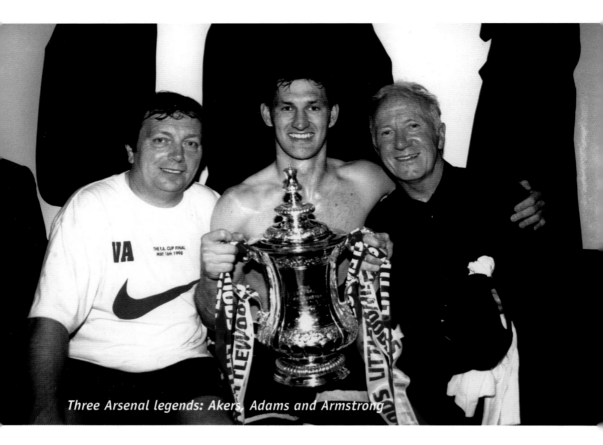

Three Arsenal legends: Akers, Adams and Armstrong

I don't think you would get any change from £15 million. Every top team would have wanted him. In the modern era the obvious comparison for Arsenal fans would be Ray Parlour for his work rate up and down the pitch in the late Nineties from the wide right.
Terry Darracott – Everton 1967-79

I think a young Ryan Giggs would be close with his box-to-box nature and skill at taking on full-backs. A 23-year-old Geordie Armstrong in his pomp would have to be worth in excess of £20 million.
Steve Stammers – Sunday Mirror

You would have to think of a player who gives his absolute all and leaves nothing on the pitch – one who works back and forth on the flank constantly, for the whole match, week in, week out. I would say James Milner, but at a higher level. Geordie would be worth £40 million, easy.
Vic Akers – Arsenal Kit Manager

I would say Frank Ribery would be similar to Geordie. Of course we did not have Pro-Zone in those days, but George could work back and forward, take on his defender, deliver accurate crosses and run all day. That would have to place his value at his peak at £30 million plus today, surely?
Gerry Peyton – Arsenal Goalkeeping coach 2003-present

It is tricky as so few modern teams in the Premier League have been playing with box-to-box wingers, so you would have to look towards Manchester United to find a comparison. Kanchelskis had the same ability to take on the full-back, but he did not have quite the same crossing ability as Geordie. Ryan Giggs, at his best, would also be a similar. For a transfer value I would say £30 to £40 million.
Frank Stapleton – Arsenal 1972-81

Is it possible to compare to a modern player? I'm not sure one exists as Geordie was an outright winger. He didn't cut in much, or shoot that often, but he could do. Geordie hugged the touchline: he did overlap, he did drift infield to help create attacks and thread passes, he had a high percentage of assists, he did track back. So perhaps he would fit in with the modern styles and I'm sure Arsene Wenger would have loved him. He isn't comparable to anyone else, he is the incomparable George 'Geordie' Armstrong who played over six hundred games for *The* Arsenal and his modern value would be priceless!
Ian Minto – Arsenal Fan

In today's market he'd be worth £40 million plus. And if Geordie had the chance to play on today's pitches at his peak I doubt there would be many that could compete. Who is there today to compare him with? Nasri? Don't make me laugh, a good player yes, but he couldn't lace Geordie's boots. Nani? I am frowning even considering it! Valencia? Stop it! The Ox? Too soon to say, but is he a winger or attacking midfielder?

Gareth Bale? It chokes me to say, but he's a great player, but he is no Geordie Armstrong and never will be. Lennon? Just a one sided, one footed Muppet. Sorry, I couldn't resist that. Only time will tell, but Cazorla, for me at least, could be a contender if he continues being played on the wing – he has two great feet and can deliver a lovely ball – but it's far too soon to compare him with Geordie. But he probably comes the closest at the moment. I'll let you know in another 500 or so matches perhaps!
Mick Wilkinson – Arsenal Fan

Comparing Geordie to a modern day player is difficult, but he had the build and two-footed qualities of Cazorla, combined with the strength and work rate of Craig Bellamy and the crossing abilities of David Beckham, yes, he was that good. Value-wise, well, I wouldn't be surprised if Geordie Armstrong, if he was here today and at his best, would be valued at between £15 and £20 million.

Pat Whelton – Arsenal Fan

It's so hard to put a price on Geordie. Every great player has a quality, skill and uniqueness about their game – whether that be a shooting, passing, heading or tackling prowess – they all determine their worth in the market. Geordie had something more though, something you can't put a price on. He was, and still is, priceless.

Des Powell – Arsenal fan

I was asked to compare Geordie to players of today and out a value on him. Impossible, he was one of a kind; priceless.

Steve Cooper – Arsenal Fan

Memory is an unreliable beast, but I see Geordie in my mind's eye as a hardscrabble, North Eastern English version of David Silva. Fast, tough, tricky, constantly buzzing around the opposition back four (or back eight, as was often the case back then).

I hear the doubting voices. "Really? David Silva? You're saying George Armstrong was that good?" Sure. Why not? How else did a 5-foot-6 winger keep his place in the (let's admit it) dour Arsenal teams of his day and rack up 621 first-team appearances? Today he'd be better protected from the likes of Ron Harris, or the entire Leeds back line. He'd also be in better condition; be thrilling fans and certainly he'd be winning England caps.

I don't know how to put a price on that, but I'll try: If Arsenal were willing to cough up £42 million for Mesut Ozil, then Geordie was worth £45 million-plus.

David Hayles – Arsenal fan

I can't liken him to a modern player at all! Wingers don't really exist as he was, let alone be able to do it on both sides of the pitch! Today's value? Phew! £30m?

Peter Stringer – Arsenal Fan

It is difficult to compare George to a modern day player or to give our younger fans an insight as to what George was like as a player. The nearest I can come up with is Ryan Giggs. The goal Giggs scored in semi final against us. I could imagine George easily doing the same. Ryan Giggs, like George, was a tireless worker with the same cocktail mix of commitment and skill. If he were playing today, I would advise the club to slap a £35 million price tag on him.
Chris Ferguson – Arsenal fan

There is nobody today who can cross a ball as accurately and he had such an unbelievable work rate. As for his value. Liverpool paid about £20m for Downing, who isn't fit to lace Geordie's boots. So I think probably somewhere in the region of £40m in today's mad transfer market I would suggest.
Gary Lawrence – Arsenal fan

I would compare him to a young Ryan Giggs. In his heyday, Geordie would go for £30 million today.
Paul Jay – Arsenal fan

For his speed, skill and crossing I would say Robert Pires, and as for value, I think into today's market Geordie would sell for £25 to £30 million.
Dennis Bedford – Arsenal fan

It is just so hard as very few can cross the ball as accurately, if any. But in today's Arsenal team, perhaps Ramsey's consistently hard work rate is a decent comparison. To value Geordie in his pomp would be around £15 million I'd say.
Stuart Stratford – Arsenal fan

BEYOND HIGHBURY: LEICESTER, VILLA AND STOCKPORT

There is no place in this book for real lows – Geordie Armstrong On The Wing is all about tributes and positive memories of a popular Arsenal legend – but there can be no doubt that leaving Highbury would unquestionably have been a low point for Geordie. Although he was very much involved in the game he loved, the 'great unknown', after spending so many years at the 'great known' would have concerned anyone. Arsenal's red and white ran through his veins as much as it did for the thousands who paid to watch him working so tirelessly for the Arsenal cause – but in the football world, and life in general, things moves on – and in August 1978 Arsenal began a top flight season without a certain George Armstrong on their payroll for the first time in 17 years. I'm hoping Geordie left the club as a player comforted by the fact that he'd been involved with the first team until the very end, missing only five games of his final season, and knowing that his teammates appreciated he would have been able to continue playing at the highest level with the Gunners for several more seasons. Not always seeing eye to eye with the new management proved decisive.

LEICESTER CITY 1977-78

Geordie's year at Leicester City [pictured left] would appear at first glance to be the result of three highly emotive decisions – the first of which was that made by Frank McLintock who, with no experience in management or coaching, accepted an offer to manage the club he'd first made his name with as a defender. The second was when McLintock decided to ask Geordie to become his first signing – the third was when Armstrong said yes. That was indeed the sequence of events but, in hindsight for all parties, perhaps it would have been better had it not been so.

McLintock had jumped at the opportunity, but he admits that, retrospectively, it was a case of heart ruling head. Frank took over a team that had finished mid-table in the 1976/77 First Division, but quickly realised that the side he'd inherited from Jimmy Bloomfield was not equipped to fight in the top flight. His best two players – Frank Worthington and Keith Weller – were sold in quick succession and he was given little money to strengthen. Whilst Liverpool, and then Manchester United, both broke the transfer record by signing Kenny Dalglish (£440,000) and Gordon McQueen (£495,000) respectively, McLintock had a less expansive budget of £150,000. With that in mind Frank opted to sign those he believed to be tried and trusted performers in the division and snapped up three friends: Geordie from Arsenal, plus Eddie Kelly and David Webb from QPR, the team from where he'd just retired as a player.

In pre-season, Leicester lost 3-0 to newly promoted Tottenham and, in McLintock's own words, the Foxes were; "Absolutely appalling." The size of the task for a novice manager now became a stark reality. After an average start, in which Geordie was in and out of the side, the team went on a run of winning just once in 26 matches – the Filbert Street outfit finished rock bottom of the table and the manager was relieved of his duties five games before the end of the season. Armstrong also suffered, for the first time in his career a series of injuries saw him miss the start of the campaign, then part of the Autumn and pre-Christmas period. Geordie only appeared in twelve matches for Leicester in that unhappy campaign and, according to both his friends, McLintock and Kelly, he never really found his feet at the club. Geordie could not reproduce the form he had shown the season before at Arsenal and, as his friend and manager said; "Perhaps even Geordie could not run that fast and be kicked that much forever."

Geordie the Fox

As well as having to deal with the selling of Leicester's top players and having little cash to find replacements, Jon Sammels, close friend to Frank and Geordie, confirmed; "it was an aging team." When Sammels was called by his new boss and old teammate, telling him he was coming to join him at Leicester – Jon told him he was about to leave. The ex-Gunner had arranged a move to Canada to finish his career with the Vancouver Whitecaps and would be off in the January. Sammels was, however, virtually ever present until he flew the nest, but has few recollections about the reasons why Geordie failed to make the expected impact at Filbert Street – aside from the aforementioned, uncharacteristic injuries. He did make one telling observation though, perhaps easy with hindsight, about the disastrous campaign. "McLintock needed one of two things in his first management role – either to have an experienced assistant alongside him – the likes of a Don Howe or, if that was not possible, an assistant he trusted who would not be afraid to tell him he was making wrong decisions or to offer hands-on advice." Given the successful coach he went on to be, Sammels suggested he should have given Geordie that role, or used him more in that capacity.

Armstrong did play frequently with the Leicester reserves, where a young Gary Lineker was about to burst on to the scene. He, and other players like the youngsters coming through at Arsenal, got the benefit of years of football wisdom and experience, even if his playing legacy was not what he may have hoped for. Geordie was not selected at all by the caretaker manager, Ian McFarlane, after McLintock was sacked, but featured in a full pre-season programme under the new permanent boss, Jock Wallace. He was then selected for a few matches of the 1978/79 campaign, before electing to take on one last playing challenge a little further north... with the Hatters of Stockport County.

STOCKPORT COUNTY 1978-79

In the summer of 1978, Mike Summerbee, undisputed Manchester City legend, and two years Geordie's senior, had been appointed player-manager at Stockport County. Summerbee had been at Edgeley Park for a season and half as a player before being asked to manage the team too, and his first signing was seen as a major coup. Nobody, including Summberbee himself, could believe that he could persuade such an iconic player to move to Stockport but, somehow, he'd convinced his old friend and sparring partner, Geordie Armstrong, to join the playing staff.

It was seen as a major signing by the County players and fans alike, and the gates rose to 8,000-10,000 as they came to see Summerbee on the right of midfield link up with Geordie on the left. Summerbee recalls the squad being given a huge lift in pre-season; "Just to train with a legend like Geordie gave the players a lift – he set a superb example to all the young players with his unfaltering appetite for training."

Even Summerbee, a veteran of over 400 matches and ten years at the top with City admits; "I found it an honour to be in the same team as Geordie after so many years admiring him as an opponent." However, despite his continual effort and application to the County cause, Geordie found it extremely difficult to adjust to Fourth Division football. The issue was that, unlike Summerbee, who had begun in the lower leagues and returned there, Geordie had only known elite football and played with elite players. The players around him simply could not control the ball or move the ball as he was used to. Worse perhaps, for Geordie, was the realisation that in Division One it was a battle of wits, skill, feint and technique between winger and full-back, whereas in the lowest division, he was just hacked crudely or hauled down.

Despite his frustrations Geordie stuck to his task and remained professional; "he never gave less than his all" admits Summerbee. Les Bradd, who had also signed with Geordie, and another veteran with 400-plus games for Notts County as a centre-forward, certainly benefited from those still perfect crosses. Armstrong, despite the physical battering, played in 34 of County's 46 League fixtures, before informing Summerbee that he intended to call time on his professional career. "I had no regrets signing Geordie" confesses Summerbee, "He was a gentleman. It's a simple as that. George was respected everywhere he went."

After Stockport, Summerbee, who says he never intended to stay in the game as a full-time coach, but he knew that his friend Geordie did. "He was taking his badges whilst at County and was keen to learn some of the coaching techniques. I'd learned from my own mentor, Malcolm Allison, who would often visit the Stockport training ground." I asked if it was this connection that later induced Allison to seek Geordie out as a coach to work with? "It is possible, but the reality was that Allison, like everybody in the game, knew Geordie already and respected his ability and his knowledge. Geordie had the skills, the ideas and the patience to work with younger, less talented players and was always destined to be a top coach. He was simply a top man. As a player you couldn't play against any better and, as a man, you wouldn't meet any finer. Geordie died too young – I miss him – as does the game of football."

ASTON VILLA -1980

When Geordie called time on his English professional playing career, from his own perspective, and as the family were by now settled in Leicester, where he'd invested in a pub in the city, more 'local' options were what the doctor ordered. Football was undoubtedly more in his blood than pulling pints, so, armed with new coaching qualifications, one of the top teams in the Midlands, indeed in the Country came calling. Ron Saunders wanted some legs and enthusiasm to assist him at Aston Villa and subsequently offered

Armstrong with the Aston Villa squad

Geordie his first break in coaching in the top flight. Some might have been daunted at the prospect but not Armstrong.

Kenny Swain – Aston Villa 1978-83

Kenny Swain is now one of the bright lights involved in the coaching set up at the Football Association and, as such, knows a thing or two about coaching young players – he is currently in charge of the England School Boys. However, he recalls Geordie as a very humble, enthusiastic coach at Villa, even in the short time he was there. "George was very popular with the close knit group, but my clearest and lasting memory is from my home debut for Chelsea in 1974. In those days I was a striker, not a full-back, and had been asked to play on the right side of Chelsea's attack – from where I scored. I was not allowed to enjoy my goal for long because, having had the ball nicked off me on the edge of Arsenal's area just afterwards, Geordie then proceed to run the whole length of the pitch, and although I chased him the whole way, he then put in a perfect cross for Kennedy to head home and equalise." Dave Sexton, the then Chelsea boss, knew all too well the danger Armstrong caused – he believed George should have been an England regular and had thoroughly briefed his team before kick-off. "Sexton's words were choice – along the lines of 'Ken what's the point of fucking tracking Armstrong back a full 70 yards if you are still going to let him put a fucking cross in?' George was a fabulous footballer."

Gordon Cowans – Aston Villa 1976-85, 1988-91 & 1993-94

Gordon Cowans is as much a legend at Aston Villa, as Geordie Armstrong is at Arsenal – enjoying around 13 years as a first team player at Villa Park with 16 years and counting on the clock as a coach. He recalled Geordie's short time as assistant to Ron Saunders with affection; "Although it was Armstrong's first senior coaching role, he had the instant respect of all the first-team squad because of what he'd achieved in the game as a player – this was further enhanced by the glowing reports they had received from Jimmy Rimmer and ex-team mate from Highbury."

Cowans recalls being astounded, along with the whole group, at just how strong Geordie was for a short guy. "He could bench press a whole stack of weights, far more than any of us!" His natural fitness was an asset as he worked closely with the team, guiding and encouraging – never needing to shout to exert his authority. When asked about the dynamic between Ron Saunders, Geordie and Tony Barton, I was surprised to hear that Barton was very much the Coaching Assistant and below Geordie in the hierarchy. One cannot help thinking of what might have been? Armstrong followed his heart and his loyal persona to Norway, whilst Aston Villa won the League title. The following season, when Ron Saunders left Villa Park, it was Tony Barton who was promoted from within – and guided Aston Villa to European glory. Could that have been Geordie if he'd stayed?

Ken McNaught – Aston Villa 1977-83

The first recollection for McNaught, as with so many others when discussing Geordie, was the fitness of the guy who was their new coach. "Ron Saunders always divided his squad into two groups for training. One group might be core work in the gym, whilst the other were doing more physical training which, in those days, meant lost of running. Armstrong would be in charge of the latter and did the session twice. He did twice as much as his players and still led from the front at all times. He was a great bloke and loved being with the players, but what came through most was his infectious personality and his complete love of football."

McNaught was also very clear that Saunders was a disciplinarian – it was always his way or the highway – and whilst the players may have loved being trained by Geordie, he was very much still one of the lads, and long-term, that may not have worked with the manager. We will never know what might have been, but what is clear, is that three Villa legends, both Division One and European Cup winners, remember their short six-month spell working with Geordie Armstrong during his first coaching position with absolute positivity.

Indeed, for Ken McNaught, even now, 34 years after Geordie left Aston Villa, he is reminded every day when he looks at his wife Maureen of his short time as coach at Villa Park. "In training one day, whilst I was gasping for breath, Geordie was talking ten to the dozen, as he did and, during the conversation, I mentioned that my wife was looking for me to buy her an 'Eternity ring.' Geordie asked what kind Maureen was looking for... So I described it to him and thought no more of it. A week later Geordie called me to one side ahead of training and opened a small box to reveal a ring, just as I'd described... "Is this the sort of thing your missus was looking for Ken?" It was as if it was the most normal thing to have done... He'd gone completely out of his way to help someone he'd only recently met and used his London connections." No questions asked, of course, but McNaught had just found out what all his team mates at Arsenal had always known. If you were a friend of Geordie Armstrong, then nothing was too much trouble.

But whilst Ron Saunders famously won the First Division tile using only 14 fantastic, yet very knackered, outfield players, George was headed much further north than the Spaghetti Junction turn-off of the M6 – the next chapter in the Armstrong story was about to unfold – and it was not a conventional one.

THE NORWEGIAN EXPERIENCE

It was a far cry from North London, or indeed Leicestershire, where Geordie had played briefly before being offered the job as assistant to Ron Saunders at Aston Villa. So how did an Arsenal legend end up seeing out his playing days and getting his real first taste of football management in a small town in the far north of Norway?

Well, if I told you the reason had something to do with Queens Park Rangers' star Stan Bowles breaking his leg, you might think I was mad... but strangely, the sequence of events began that way. It all starts with a mysterious Norwegian footballer-come-entrepreneur by the name of Jack Anderson *[pictured above with Frank McLintock]*.

Back in the spring of 1977 Jack, of FK Mjølner, had been in London looking for big name English talent to play in a tournament he was planning in Norway. He was hoping to create a Mjølner All Stars XI to play matches against other Norwegian sides. He had attended a Fulham match, ostensibly to watch Best and Marsh, but had left unimpressed. He wanted real players, not show-boaters. During a chance taxi ride a cabbie told him that he knew Frank McLintock and, as well as playing, he ran a pub called the Sutton Arms, which he could take him to. As most Gunners will know their former skipper had invested in the pub after his playing career.

The Sutton Arms was duly visited and deal was done with Big Frank, who had just announced his retirement from playing with QPR – a lucrative offer that involved McLintock and his team mate Stan Bowles travelling to Narvik in Norway for a two-week, all-expenses-paid holiday and appearance money for two matches for Anderson's Mjølner All Stars, who would be playing Narvik and Tromsø.

A few weeks later, however, Bowles broke his leg and Frank had to ring Jack to discuss what to do. McLintock explained that, for the money on offer, he could probably convince any top player, but he had already spoken to his old Arsenal team mate, George Armstrong, who was keen to step into Stan's boots. Geordie was accepted readily and the two travelled to Narvik and, it was that May that a friendship between Jack and Geordie was cemented, one which was to endure for the remainder of the Englishman's life. But it was to become significant far sooner.

It was whilst in Narvik for that two-week tournament in Spting 1977 that McLintock was to take a call, witnessed by Jack and Geordie, in which he was offered the manager's job at Leicester City, with Frank then making Geordie, one of his closest friends and a player he knew so well, his first signing as a manager.

Anderson, like so many, had fallen under the spell of the charismatic and engaging Geordie and, for the next few years, always stayed in touch with the Armstrong family in Leicester when he visited England. Indeed, in the summer 1978, Geordie helped Anderson take Liam Brady and Frank Stapleton over to Mjølner for the next All Stars event.

Due to injuries, Anderson had started to play less at Mjølner and in the Norwegian close season, the winter of 1980, he was been asked by the club, with his connections and all, whether he could suggest a candidate with the experience and enthusiasm to take on the manager's job and elevate the club to the next level.

By that stage Geordie was coaching under Ron Saunders at Aston Villa, a side that was embarked on a course to win the League title, but he was convinced by Anderson to take on the job in Norway and, as a consequence, he moved his young family to Narvik – one of the most Northernmost towns in the worlds and 140 miles inside the Arctic Circle – to begin a new life as

FK Mjølner: The Gaffer

manager of FK Mjølner. It may have been the Norwegian Second Division, with a largely amateur squad, but Geordie took to the task with his usual gusto.

Geordie enjoyed a full pre-season with his new squad, ahead of a League campaign that began in March, and despite having ceased playing in England, his phenomenal fitness levels saw him virtually ever-present as player manager. His assistant was a player-coach called Dagfinn Rognmo, a man who went on to succeed Geordie at Mjølner, before a hugely successful career as a coach, in which he won the Norwegian Cup with Tromsø in 1986.

Another player in Armstrong's side was a young Per-Mathias Hogmo, who was at university studying to become a teacher whilst playing football as a striker for Mjølner – he was in the welcoming party, with the Chairman, that met Geordie and his family at the airport. Hogmo is currently the Norwegian national coach, having previously taken the Norway women's side to Olympic glory in Sydney and to fourth place in the World Cup a year earlier. Both, inevitably, will tell you they learned from their time with Geordie Armstrong.

It would be fair to say, that even at the age of 36, Geordie led by example and his infectious enthusiasm and winning mentality rubbed off on his players. As Anderson recalled; "Virtually every training session concluded with a five-a-side, but training was not finished until the team he was playing in were winning. He was a player and the referee, and a hugely biased one at that, but his team loved him for it and always worked with a smile on their faces."

Per-Mathias Hogmo takes the story up... "The initial reaction to the news was simple incredulity. An Arsenal hero, who had won the League and the FA Cup was going to play and be the new manager of Mjølner – it was too good to be true. The emotions were those of anticipation and excitement, not just among the players and staff but in the town of Narvik itself."

George, his wife Marj, Jill and Tom arrived in Narvik, the home of FK Mjølner, in the first week of February. It was a very cold day, with the temperature hovering around minus 20 degrees and Rogmno suspects they were ill-prepared for the conditions – and he would be right. Marj admitted that, "an anorak from England, which is what we were all wearing, is not an anorak fit for Norway!"

Rognmo says that recruiting George Armstrong as the player-manager for FK Mjølner set out a new agenda for the development the club – beforehand coaches had always been promoted from within – but the signing of George was intended to take the club on an upward spiral to a higher level of Norwegian football.

The club was largely amateur with all the players fitting in training around their jobs, but Armstrong made every minute he had with his new players count. Rognmo suggests that other British coaches had arrived in Norway prior to Geordie but, on reflection, most had done so to pick up a pay cheque for as little effort and possible. Geordie was the complete opposite, preparing meticulously for every training session and every match – always knowing what the learning outcomes should be for his new charges.

Before arriving, Armstrong had told the club that he expected the players to be physically fit, which meant the players had to begin their pre-season preparation in the November, so Geordie took over quite content with their physical standard – the Englishman was, however, very surprised about the training conditions.

During the winter all training took place outdoors on hard-packed snow. Rognmo explains; "Because of the frozen ground, the player's football boots had sharp steel knobs; George called them 'daggers' and was not very happy about using them in training and matches – he also initially took issue with the fact that everyone played with hats on. Geordie was less than impressed. 'How can you head a ball with a hat on?' he would say." He soon adapted to the weather and the necessities of football in Norway though.

More importantly, to achieve success at the club, Geordie had to get to grips with the reality of its professionalism, the economics and of the limited facilities. "He adapted to these conditions and understood the restrictions he had to work within compared to clubs he'd experienced in England swiftly..." according to Rognmo. Armstrong did, nevertheless, impose a new kind of professionalism on the team. "With his strong character and wealth of experience he set an example and created a more serious attitude to the game among the players both on and off the field."

Having not played professionally since May 1979, Geordie got his boots back on in earnest that pre-season and played in all 11 matches, scoring three times. The Norwegian season runs from March to November, with a mid season interlude, and by early March, Geordie had knocked his new team into some sort of readiness for the season ahead.

Despite his qualities as a coach and a leader, his biggest immediate impact was as a player – on the field Geordie took command with a repertoire of high class passing and unwavering enthusiasm and FK Mjølner found themselves competing among the top sides of their league and were in with a chance of qualifying for the First League in Norway all through his first season. Mjølner eventually finished fourth in the Second League that year, but standards and results had improved.

George Armstrong and Dagfinn Rogmno became close friends and spent a lot of time together – Rogmno soaking up the knowledge his friend loved to impart; "George had fantastic experience as a player. Being one of Arsenal's most consistent players for so many years had taught him an incomprehensible amount and I think I was a good listener to what he told me. I bombarded him with questions and he gave me a memory for life."

In the early weeks of that first season Rogmno revealed how Geordie gradually imposed his new regime having assessed what he had. "There would be

No hats please – its just not British

hard work to be successful but it was not the physical side but the football skills side he needed to address most. Some of the attributes he expected and required were lacking and the primary elements he wanted to introduce quickly was a maximum of two touches on the ball with faster passing."

Rogmno remembers the message was delivered with such enthusiasm and belief by Geordie, but it was not well received by a few of the players. "There were three or four who had built their game on running and dribbling with the ball, but Geordie was firm and encouraging, he convinced the players that to improve their skill and their results, they had to move the ball faster. He was right."

Listening to Rogmno it seems evident that Geordie had learned much from the Arsenal success he had been a part of, especially from the likes of Mee and Howe regarding the art of producing success collectively and building a great team work ethic.

"George was easy to like. He had great charisma and he cared. He was eager to make us better individuals, but the goal was to create a better team. He was a team builder. Very often he stressed the importance of the spirit in the team, to have faith in each other and to be a team the fans could see had players who were fighting for one and another."

Geordie, according to his Norwegian assistant, had a particular knack for improving the younger players and was skilled in knowing the right moment to encourage them, give them credit and confidence. I feel Rogmno has identified a theme that was born at Arsenal when Armstrong was a player, but also highlights his giving nature – the unique trait that would feature throughout his coaching career.

The word that is used continuously by the current Head of Norwegian football when discussing his friend and mentor is 'inspirational.' "He inspired the club to a greater level of professionalism and opened the eyes of all the players to international football." In short, Armstrong brought the football of a more advanced football nation to northern Norway when it came to training methods and tactics for matches. For Hogmo, his 16 months with Geordie awakened him to the possibility of combining a love of education and teaching, with his passion for football – and an altogether new career path. "To be honest I will always have great memories of my time in football but when I look back George was one of the great inspirations in my life."

Geordie, however, was not just an inspiration in training, or just as a manager, but he led by example on the pitch too, barely missing a game in his time at FK Mjølner. With Hogmo being a centre-forward, one might have assumed that he would be the one to get on the end of a guaranteed, steady supply of trademark Armstrong crosses? However, whilst he may have taken corners and free kicks, he explained that Geordie, as player-manager, had positioned himself in the centre of the midfield, from here he could dictate and observe the play.

Hogmo remembers another salient football lesson, learned in an away match at Kvek Halden. "The team was struggling to break down the opposition and I found myself drifting deeper and deeper trying to find space. At half-time I was greeted with some direct advice from the manager; "For fuck's sakes Per, stay up front and take the fight to those centre-backs. Show them you are a man!""

That day was just one of many where Geordie made the other players see the bigger team picture and it changed Hogmo's attitude to his role within the team. Of course Armstrong worked hard with him to give him and the team the tools, but it was all about being prepared, being on the front foot, then executing those plans with speed and precision.

Both Rogmno and Hogmo, though at different stages of their careers – the former a senior player already looking to learn as a coach, the latter a young players still finding his way in the game – clearly feel indebted to Geordie Armstrong. He inspired both to embrace the preparation and professionalism. How many more would be inspired by the great man?

Oistein Kristoffersen was not just an avid supporter of FK Mjølner in the early Eighties, he was also the Kit Manager whilst Armstrong was in charge of the club... as well as following Arsenal since the 1960s, when Geordie had

Geordie proves he's still got it in Norway

broken into the team. I guess Kristoffersen was FK Mjølner's equivalent to Vic Akers at Arsenal today – and somebody who was present at virtually every game of Geordie's tenure in Norway.

Kristoffersen described the huge anticipation of everyone involved with the club once they learned that one of England's finest was coming to Navik to manage at their small club. "The standard was obviously not as high as he was used to, but I witnessed how swiftly he had them organized and playing his way and how, with little fuss, managed the ones who were lazy or not buying into his vision."

"Geordie's training sessions were always high intensity but fun – there was always laughter ringing around the training ground." Kristoffersen also recalls Geordie making the players take their hats off when it was minus 15 degrees and insisting 'you can't play football with fucking hats on!' That soon changed!" Kristoffersen says with a smile.

"From the touchline looking on, Geordie was obviously the best player in training and in matches, but he used this in a positive fashion by demonstrating and encouraging. He was always giving the players the belief that they could improve and he never criticized or shouted at them."

Geordie put Mjølner on the map, increased the fan base and, because English football was so popular in Norway, was famous everywhere he went. Kristoffersen says that even at away games, opposition fans, and even players, would ask for Geordie's autograph.

One of Geordie's endearing traits was, that despite being a winner who hated losing, and obviously knew more than anyone at the club, he was still happy to listen and take opinions on board from colleagues. This was important for a player-manager, especially with Dagfinn being his player-coach, and Geordie sometimes requested a touchline perspective from either Kristoffersen, or the other Kit Man, Geir Indragaard. One match he remembers, though, was particularly amusing.

It was an important game where FK Mjølner had to win to keep in touch with the leading teams. During the half time break, with the score at 1-1, Geordie clearly told Kristoffersen that any change would have to take place in accordance to his instructions. However, the other team took the lead with only ten minutes to go and Geordie had not made any changes as yet, so Kristoffersen made the decision to put on a forward... but the substitution was not according to Geordie's instructions. The player he introduced proceeded to score twice and win the game. Afterward the Kit Man described how he went to Armstrong and apologised for making a change not approved in advance, or as instructed... "Geordie turned and looked at me with a wide smile and said; 'Fuck you Oistein!'"

Geordie left FK Mjølner half way through the second season, but it was not a case that he or his family, who by that stage were settled into the Norwegian way of life, were unhappy or had been thinking of a return to

England. Marj's father had passed away and Geordie's wife, understandably, wanted to return home to be near her mother. Back in 1981 international airports had not sprung up everywhere, meaning quick visits back home were simply not possible, especially from that far north. It was an hour and a half's train trip to Evenes, then a two-hour internal flight to Oslo, then another two hour-plus flight just to get back to London – let alone the next leg of the trip up to the North East of England. But, despite his premature departure, Geordie had left FK Mjølner in a fair better shape than he'd found it and the Armstrong family left Norway having forged lifelong friendships.

Geordie had also inspired at least two of his players to embark on successful coaching careers of their own, as Rogmno underlines. "I learned from George, so much more than I was able to see in July 1981, when he left. There is no doubt, though, that he inspired me to continue coaching for more than 20 years. Everyone who worked with George at FK Mjølner learned to know a person with integrity and a great personality. He will always be remembered fondly in FK Mjølner's history book."

The successful, winning football under Armstrong saw a lowly FK Mjølner side reach their highest ever position, third in the second tier, and attendances more than trebled from an average of 1,500 a week to around 5,000. Geordie had played 53 matches for FK Mjølner, scoring nine goals in the process and played his last game in Norway on July 5, 1981. In handing over the management of the club to Rogmno, with a new professional ethic and with players and staff primed to continue his good work, he'd left the club in good shape and Geordie would be delighted to know that the people of Narvik still remember the Armstrong family with much affection to this day.

WEST LONDON TO WEST LONDON VIA MIDDLESBROUGH

O n arriving back in England in the summer of 1981, Geordie was to be reunited with his old Arsenal team mate of the 1976/77 season, Malcolm Macdonald. Super Mac, as he was affectionately known, had returned to Craven Cottage, where he'd played previously, as manager and had helped them secure mid-table in the third tier. It was hoped that 1981/82 was to be the season to push on and win promotion to Division Two and Macdonald obviously felt the energy and experience of Geordie was what was needed before installing him as his first team coach. Who better to recall the impact Armstrong made with the first team at Fulham than the man between the sticks for the West London club from 1977 to 1986, and who is now a coach at Arsenal himself, Gerry Peyton.

"I love professional people and Geordie was the capital 'P' of Profes-sional." says Peyton, whose initial memory of Geordie as a coach, although he had played against him, was the first day of pre-season training, when he took the whole squad on a seven-mile run around Richmond Park. "Armstrong started the run with us at the front, then, halfway round, he ran all the way to the back to encourage the stragglers before running past everyone back to the front and finished first." Geordie was nearly 38 at that stage. "The reality was that Geordie and Macdonald were still the best two footballers at Fulham. In training Geordie would ping crosses in and Macdonald would finish them. And when the manager asked Geordie to cross the ball so the 'Mitre' logo was on his forehead, the players all thought he was joking, but Geordie did it. He could direct a cross onto a player's chest, head or for a volley on request!" Peyton recalls.

He also remembers how the players all enjoyed working with Geordie and particularly how the full-backs and wide players' crossing ability and accu-racy improved under his tutelage. "He would spend ages with those players showing them the benefits of crossing a moving ball on the run. His sessions were always hard work and Geordie had a huge belief in the work ethic, but he always ensured the right blend of fun was present."

Peyton admired Geordie as a coach and as a person – another fellow professional who found him to be exceptionally straight talking and honest. Peyton emphasises this point, describing Geordie as a man of high morals and principles. "There are very few people you meet as you travel through your career in this game that you instantly think, this is a fantastic person."

Peyton will never forget the one season he worked with Armstrong at Fulham. The club narrowly missed out on back-to-back promotions and, for reasons only known to Macdonald and not understood by any of the players, Geordie did not return for the next pre-season. "The senior professionals loved working with him and the younger players at Fulham were just in awe of him." Peyton described Geordie as; "Someone who just loved the game of football, every aspect of it. He was a football purist, but every day you worked with him, you just knew he was a winner and wanted to win."

It might be argued by some that Macdonald had promoted Ray Harford to replace Geordie, perhaps because he felt threatened by his assistant's popularity. It was ironic then, that when he was sacked some 18 months later, it was Harford who happily stepped into his manager's shoes without remorse. Something, as Geordie's next adventure will demonstrate, he would not have done himself. Loyalty was hard-wired into Geordie's DNA, and whilst being true to his code of conduct may have cost him professionally, his honour remained intact wherever his went in the game.

Years later, Peyton was delighted that his path crossed with Geordie again on two occasions in successive seasons while he was a 'keeper at Everton. The first time came in 1992 when Peyton was loaned to Norwich City, where he played in a reserve team match against Geordie's Arsenal; "I played a blinder and Norwich won 1-0. Geordie came to find me afterwards and congratulated me on a good display – I was delighted to see him."

"The following season, following an injury to Dave Beasant, Everton loaned me to Chelsea, where I again found myself lining up against Geordie's Arsenal reserves. I played well again and kept a clean sheet in a 1-0 win. Once more Geordie came to find me and congratulate me, after which he said; "Fucking hell Gerry, next time you get offered to go out on loan, whoever it is for, can you make sure they are not due to play the Arsenal!""

TROWBRIDGE & ENDERBY

In the few months in between leaving Fulham there was a little-publicised outing or two for an old friend at Trowbridge Town. Geordie would have met Alan Birchenall on many occasions during his playing career, playing against him with Sheffield United, Chelsea, Crystal Palace and Leicester City. As Geordie was arriving at Leicester City in 1977, Birchenall was heading through the out door, to play for Notts County, but he still lived in the Leicester area and often had a drink with Geordie and another mutual friend, Jon Sammels.

By the summer of 1982, Birchenall had become player-manager at Trowbridge Town, where he'd performed miracles in taking them through the non-League divisions to the then Alliance Premier. However, he had a young side and staying in the division, which is the equivalent of today's Conference was going to be a stiff challenge. The timing coincided with a period that Geordie was at a slight lose end. Birchenall tells the story; "We were in the pub one night and I asked Geordie if he fancied keeping fit until something concrete came along – would he be interested in turning out for me at Trowbridge? The response was along the lines of 'Where the hell is Trowbridge 'Birch'?' 'In Wiltshire, Geordie'…. 'And where's that?' he joked."

Geordie agreed, but the amusement did not end there though, as Birchenall had unwittingly combined possibly the oldest and most experienced midfield in non-League football history; "Taking to the field for the first game of the season, against the 'giants' of the division, Kettering Town, was an incredible array of talent. We may not find this in any record books, but we lined up from left to right in midfield: Geordie Armstrong, aged 38, with around 650 professional appearances for Arsenal, Leicester City and Stockport County. Centre-mid, Alan Birchenall, aged 36, circa 500 professional appearances for Sheffield United, Chelsea, Crystal Palace, Leicester and Notts County. Centre-mid, Jon Sammels, aged 37, 550-plus professional appearances for Arsenal and Leicester City. Right-mid, Trevor Tainton, a youngster at just 34, but with over 500 professional appearances for Bristol City. The team talk before the first match was 'Right lads, let's not give the ball away cheaply, because looking at the combined age of our midfield, we will never win it back!'"

But in all seriousness, according to Birchenall, Geordie was still flying all over the pitch and the most hard-working player in the team, which put the rest of them to shame. "It was great while it lasted, but it was only a handful of games and, even in that short time, I used Geordie as a player-coach such was his knowledge and tactical acumen."

Geordie cut short his time with Trowbridge Town when his local non-League side came-a-calling and his first spell as a manager in England came at Enderby Town, who later became Leicester United, but are now no longer in existence. Details of his tenure are understandably hard to come by but Armstrong once described it; "... as a refreshing contrast to the pressures of the big time." However, at the end of that 1982/83 season, 'Mr Big Time' himself got in touch.

MIDDLESBROUGH

After his one-year stint by the river in West London and season-long sojourn in non-League management, Geordie's football roller-coaster made its way North-East again, but not quite as far as Hebburn, where his adventures had all started. Geordie knew that if he was serious about coaching, and being the best he could be, he needed to continue learning from the best – so when he received a phone call from Malcolm Allison inviting him to become his first-team coach at Middlesbrough, there was only ever likely to be one answer from Geordie. Although, as it transpired, I am not really sure who learned from whom?

As we learned earlier, Malcolm Allison had watched Geordie working with Mike Summerbee, one of his prodigies, whilst at Stockport County, however, in digging a little deeper, I discovered Allison's admiration of Geordie was long standing. In 1972, when interviewed by the late David Coleman for his *World of Football* book, this was his view of the then Arsenal winger. "George Armstrong: the player the professionals admire. He is a tremendous worker. He's there when it breaks down, he's back upsetting players, he's making runs, and he uses everything he's got." To give that context, we should bear in mind that when Allison said that of Armstrong, he'd just guided Manchester City to a League title, an FA Cup, then a Cup Winners' Cup and League Cup double in successive seasons from 1968 to 1970 – he was considered one of the finest and most innovative football coaches in the game.

Middlesbrough, however, were a club in financial crisis – gates were down at Ayresome Park and the club were losing big money. Perhaps that was not the ideal backdrop for the new management team, but, to get a real picture of the situation in which Geordie was dropped head-first, I spoke with a man who barely missed a game for 'Boro between 1982 and 1984.

Mick Kennedy had arrived in the summer of 1982, signed from Huddersfield Town by Allison's predecessor, Bobby Murdoch. Within months of his arrival, in the September, Murdoch was shown the door, and within two months, Malcolm Allison was announced as Middlesbrough's new Manager. Kennedy explained that; "The players had little idea what to expect, other than, perhaps, the unexpected. The first big news came a few weeks later when Malcolm announced he was bringing in Geordie Armstrong as his first team coach."

Allison then proceeded to drop, or sell, most of the existing first-teamers as he looked to build a team using the existing young talent at the club. There is no question that Allison had done this before, but one suspects that, on this occasion, it had more to do with the financial constraints imposed rather than his belief in the youngsters at 'Boro. Either way, it was obvious from the very beginning that Allison was going to leave it all to Geordie, barring match-days.

There were only about three or four regular first-teamers who were older than their early 20s and, to emphasise just how tough it was as the season progressed, Kennedy describes the official team photo he has on his wall at home, taken during the pre-season of 1983/84; "The photo shows Malcolm Allison in an old Manchester City tracksuit, Geordie in some tatty old top that looks like it was purchased from the market." It was under this cash-strapped backdrop that Geordie got to work with his young squad and, to Kennedy's mind, worked miracles. Stephen Bell, a talented left-winger was 17; striker David Currie, 20; Tony Mowbray, 19; Darren Wood, full-back, 18; Kelham O'Hanlon, the goalie, 20; is to name just a few according to Kennedy – but all would feel indebted to Geordie. Most of them, of course, had watched him play at his peak for Arsenal on television as children, but the respect they had from that just grew and grew.

"As far as the young players were concerned, Geordie ran the whole club. They rarely saw Malcolm Allison, but Geordie was ever-present. He set up training, took every session, laid out their kits on match-days and even followed the small coach to games in his own car. He was the first to arrive every morning and the last to leave at night. After the match on a Saturday, Geordie would drive back to his family home, then be back bright and early every Monday morning. They youngsters all felt they could go to him with their problems and nothing was ever too much trouble. Everybody knew how hard he worked and how much he did for the young players – there was a total and utter respect for him. The lads were not used to a coach who would 'get a sweat on' with them or somebody who could demonstrate anything he wanted them to know." For Kennedy, in a long an illustrious career, he had never met a man he respected more. "I loved him and the young lads knew if they stepped out of line for Geordie they would have to answer to me! However, that rarely happened because all the youngsters saw how much Geordie put in for them... Even the senior professionals, players like Heini Otto, a 'Boro legend, bought into the Armstrong way. The reality was, that to most of them in that period, Geordie Armstrong *was* Middlesbrough Football Club..." But Kennedy doubts many outside the place knew that.

What he is certain of is that all the young professionals who broke through under Geordie owe him a great deal. Kennedy feels that to steer a team to safety, with no money and six or seven first-team regulars aged under 20 during that era was nothing short of a miracle – a miracle that was down to Geordie far more than Allison.

Kennedy admits his affections towards Malcolm Allison too, and that he found him an inspiration on match-days, but it was Armstrong who ensured the youngsters were honed and prepared. Despite Allison seemingly being mostly absent, that was only possible due to the complete trust he had in Armstrong to do the job, or so it seemed to Kennedy. "There was evidently huge admiration from Allison toward his coach and, in return, Armstrong was loyal to his mentor and learned from him on match days."

Whilst Allison was a superb motivator, it was Geordie the players trusted. Kennedy describes an uncanny ability to tread the line of being their coach, and simultaneously, one of the lads. "Quite often, in fact more often than not, the changing room was the players' sanctuary and coaches knew to stay out at times. Geordie was like a shadow and the players were content for him to move around amongst them, safe in the knowledge that nothing would get back to Allison. There was no bawling or shouting from Geordie. He had so much patience with us and I don't remember him even having to raise his voice."

Kennedy worked with many respected football people including Jack Charlton, Malcolm Allison, Ray Harford and Alan Ball in a career spanning ten clubs and over 600 matches, but no-one earned his respect in the way that Geordie Armstrong did. Alan Ball, who managed Kennedy at his next club, Portsmouth, felt the same way about Geordie. "If Bally was in a good mood after a win, I would often have long football conversations and Geordie was mentioned on several occasions – I was left in no doubt that Alan had the same huge regard for Armstrong as I did."

When Allison was sacked for being too outspoken in the Press about the sale of Darren Wood to Chelsea in the Spring of 1984, Geordie, perhaps too loyal for once, elected to follow. Kennedy felt that he did not have to do so and all the squad were hugely disappointed to see him leave Ayresome Park. "George was a true gentleman of football, he was respected by all in the game I imagine. When I heard of his death, I was heartbroken."

Tony Mowbray – Middlesbrough 1982-91

As Kennedy suggested, the financial pressures had caused the club to sell most of the established players and Allison integrated many young players – Tony Mowbray was one of the lucky local lads. Looking back, he assumes the veteran Manager, as Allison was considered, needed an energetic, enthusiastic assistant to work with these fledging pros.

Allison, by this stage of his career, was not at all active on the training pitch, and it was Geordie who endeavoured to ready the players for matches and maintain their belief under very difficult circumstances, serving as the intermediary between the manager and the players, who all loved him. Mowbray recalls; " Geordie was always jovial, full of beans and always there for a chat and ready with advice."

The constant enthusiasm was impressive as Mowbray feels that; "He must have been so frustrated at the quality of some of the players he had to work with, but he was always encouraging the young players – there with an arm around them, picking them up and rebuilding fragile confidence." In reality it was a relegation battle for the players, with no reserves, or experience to draw upon in the main, so Geordie's presence was invaluable. Mowbray continues; "I had huge respected for Geordie. He was highly thought of by us all and, in a very difficult time in the club's history, he was a ray of sunshine."

One interesting postscript to Geordie's season back in the North-East was that, given the two teams were in different divisions, Middlesbrough and Arsenal met on three occasions in a year, twice just before his arrival (1982/83), but once with him as coach. Geordie's spiritual club were drawn away at Ayersome Park on 1983/84 FA Cup Third Round day – January 3, 1984.

Arsenal, unbeaten in five games under Don Howe since the departure of Terry Neill, arrived in Middlesbrough brimming with internationals – but Sansom, Jennings, Nicholas, Woodcock, O'Leary and Rix were to find themselves humbled 3-2 by Geordie's kids. One can only wonder at the mixed emotions felt by Geordie that day, but I can certainly guess he felt immensely proud of his part in outwitting his old mentor and coach, Howe.

Sadly, within a matter of weeks, Allison's outbursts during a Press conference, that followed a midweek defeat, left the board with no choice other to sack him. His departure gave the newspapers headlines such as 'It is better to die than face a long lingering death' and 'Middlesbrough has five or six weeks to live.' Allison's outspokenness and high profile, champagne lifestyle had cost him his job as well as Armstrong's.

It is perhaps strange that the loyalty felt by Geordie towards Allison, given the incongruous nature of their personalities and work ethic, but as we shall discover, it would not be long until they were back riding the same tandem.

QPR

After a short break, Geordie found himself back in West London, this time at the request of newly-installed Queens Park Rangers manager and England legend, Alan Mullery. Geordie was brought in as part of the regime that had been tasked with the almost impossible job of replacing Terry Venables, who'd recently been head-hunted by Barcalona.

During a short, five-month spell, one that Mullery describes as; "The worst job of my career", Geordie kept his head down, working with the reserves and youths, while is boss struggled with a Chairman and a first team that simply had not come to terms with losing El Tel. Ultimately, Mullery was unable to make changes and was confronted by resistance at every turn, which clearly made his position untenable. By the Christmas, Mullery and most of his staff were gone – Geordie remained until February.

The short period was again characterised by the energy and enthusiasm synonymous with Geordie working with young players – both as a player and a coach – and not just the training pitch. Geordie found himself playing fairly regularly in the reserves whilst some of younger lads, who had been disciplined, were demoted back to youth team matches.

In the November and December of his 40th year, Geordie played for QPR reserves five times and was not on the losing side. In his own words; "I think it has been useful to the other lads. When you are coaching kids you can show them more in a few seconds during a match than in hours of training." Geordie played himself at full-back, still fit enough to cope, whilst using his expert knowledge to counter the threat from the wing.

If there was any doubt he was still a winner, even at that ripe age as a player, a quietly-shared moment with his son Tom would dispel that. "After his first outing for QPR reserves, against Ipswich, he told me how proud he was to have marked the (then) full Irish International winger, Kevin O'Callaghan, out of the game... "I never gave him a kick!""

Geordie's incredible fitness and an ability to be hands on with the players had come to his aide once again – it is yet another example of his refreshing coaching style that so many players that he worked with found their football education so invaluable. I was able to catch up briefly with a couple of the QPR lads.

Gavin Maguire (QPR 1984-89)

Gavin was a Youth Team player who had the opportunity to work with Geordie and he recalls a few players wondering why the coach was picking himself and not promoting them; "But they soon realised how much he had to offer the team and how much they could learn from just watching and playing alongside him." Maguire's main recollection of his brief period of being coached by Geordie was how the seemingly unlimited energy and enthusiasm just rubbed off on everyone around him. "He could certainly appear gruff and no nonsense, but he was nice at the same time, which is quite a trick!"

John Byrne (QPR 1984-88)

Byrne was one of the few notable signings made by Mullery, the deal coming after QPR had played against Fourth Division York City in the League Cup. Having arrived at Loftus Road, Byrne found himself spending a short time with Geordie, whilst waiting for a chance to break into the first team. "Geordie left shortly after I arrived, but I just remember what a genuinely nice person he was. I was just a young kid, newly signed from York, and he was extremely kind and welcoming to me."

It may have been an awful time for Alan Mullery but, as usual, Geordie left Loftus Road with his reputation for coaching young and inexperienced players augmented. But the next challenge was going to be about as far removed from English football as he might have dreamt possible.

THE KUWAIT ADVENTURE

A chapter that covers Geordie's time in Kuwait was always going to be tricky to write as, mysteriously, the source material and all records of his time there have either been hidden or have disappeared altogether. This could be explained because Armstrong's successful, and largely happy, time in Kuwait did not end well, indeed, his departure, just as the Gulf War was about to kick-off, was hastened further because of a dispute with those that ran Salmiya – the club he was managing in 1990.

A dispute over unfair dismissal and unpaid wages was settled in Geordie's favour after FIFA had become involved, by which time he was settled back in the bosom of his Arsenal family, however, the nature of his exit from Kuwait should not over shadow his achievements in the oil rich state. As I alluded, it would seem that much of his presence has sadly been erased from the records in Kuwait, but there are medals, letters and certificates in the family's possession, as well as family memories that should allow us to do some justice to Geordie's second international adventure. This time somewhere where the climate would ensure there would certainly be no excuses about the need to wear bobble hats in training, that's for sure!

In the summer of 1985 Geordie was reunited with his boss from Middlesbrough when he joined Malcolm Allison, who had been invited out to Kuwait to work with the national side. Obviously football in Kuwait, both at national and at club level, was very different at the time, with all the control resting with individual families or Sheiks and, to a degree, Armstrong was heading into the unknown. Having said that, many British coaches had already successfully followed the oil dollar by accepting the challenge of raising the standard of Kuwaiti football, and two of those already there, were old friends of Geordie's – Dave Mackay, his old North London sparring partner, and Bobby Campbell, a coach he'd worked with at Arsenal during the 1970s.

Geordie initially went out with his colleagues and his son, Tom, but they found themselves with long periods of inactivity whilst the national team players were with their clubs – the first fixture was a home match with Mexico and their new charges held their vastly more experienced opponents to a credible 0-0 draw. However, the main purpose of bringing in a top foreign management team was to restore national pride and regain the Gulf Cup.

The prestigious competition, held bi-annually between the Gulf nations, had seen Kuwait victorious on five of the first six occasions between 1970 until 1982, however, in 1984, under the management of Antonio Lopes, the Kuwait team had not just lost the title to Iraq, but they had been humiliated. Finishing in sixth place when there are only seven nations participating, and winning just one match, was totally unacceptable for a nation that under another great Brazilian, Carlos Alberto Parreira, had made the World Cup finals in Spain two years earlier where they had lost 1-0 to England in their final group phase thanks to a Trevor Francis goal.

The period of inactivity, between the October international and the Gulf Cup in the March of 1986, saw Geordie training personally each day and being available to work with any Kuwait player, international or otherwise, who wanted to learn or be coached by him. If he was not on the training pitch he would be found running or playing tennis. His work ethic, whilst his colleagues stayed in the hotel, was seemingly observed by those who ran the Football Federation as, early in 1986, three of the four English staff were dismissed, whilst Armstrong was asked to stay to coach the Kuwait team alongside Saleh Zakaria, a Kuwaiti Manager, who had briefly had the role in 1978. Until that point, as we have read, Geordie would have resigned (again) when Malcolm Allison was relieved of his duties, but this time, in Kuwait, Geordie elected to stay and look after himself and his family.

Armstrong was enjoying life in Kuwait and the challenge of trying to mould the young Kuwaiti team into winners again was an irresistible one. On

Geordie receives the royal seal of approval in Kuwait

the eve of their departure for the tournament, which was to be held in Bahrain, Geordie and Zakaria's team took on Iceland in a friendly, home fixture during which their veteran striker, Faisal Al-Dakhil, scored the only goal. The team departed to compete for the Gulf Cup in good spirits and in confident mood.

The Gulf Cup of 1986 began on March 23 and concluded on April 7, during which time all seven nations – Kuwait, Iraq, Quatar, Saudi Arabia, UAE, Bahrain and Oman – played each other in the usual round robin format. Geordie's players did him proud, losing and drawing on just one occasion and winning the other four matches. They played attacking, attractive football, scored 11 goals, and conceded just four – Kuwait had won the tournament by four clear points.

The team were flown home aboard the Sheik's private jet where thousands of people were awaiting their arrival – including Marj and Jill – at Kuwait City Airport. I am told the interior of the aeroplane was predominantly 'gold.' Armstrong had achieved hero status in Kuwaiti and, with his stock so high, was confident other offers would be forthcoming. He was missing the day-to-day involvement with players and thought his immediate future lay away from the national team.

That summer Geordie was recommended for the manager's job at Al Arabi, one of the giants of the Kuwaiti league, by his old friend Dave Mackay, who was leaving to coach in Dubai, so Geordie found himself inheriting that role for the 1986/87 season. Despite winning four successive titles between 1981 and 1985, Arabi had fallen off the pace and had finished third in Mackay's last season there. The new job kept Geordie in Kuwait City, in a comfortable community, surrounded by other British coaches and their families.

Geordie found he was able to take Arabi forward, and despite only finishing as runners-up, Armstrong's hands-on coaching saw the side win nine times in the 12 league games. It was a big leap forward for the club compared to just five wins in the previous campaign.

Unfortunately, though, Geordie's success may well have been disadvantageous for his old Arsenal coach and friend, Bobby Campbell. Campbell was the coach at Al Qadisa, the other big club in the capital – in 1985/86 he had taken them close and finished second – but in 1986/87, whilst Geordie improved Arabi, Qadsia dropped down to a fourth-place finish.

It was to cost Campbell his job and that of his assistant, a young, up-and-coming English coach finding his way having retired early as a player. His name was Malcolm Crosby and, after just one year, he and his family were facing the prospect of returning to the UK.

Crosby, currently Chief Scout at Birmingham City, was just 33 and the role with Campbell had been his first senior role after embarking on a coaching career that had started back home with York City. As he explained to me, in the first few weeks after arriving in Kuwait, his family were finding it hard to settle, until they met Geordie and Marj at a party.

"I obviously knew about Geordie's achievements as a player with Arsenal and I was surprised how modest he was and how he really wanted to talk and get to know me better."

Almost immediately Crosby felt he had a strong bond with Geordie and the two coaches, along with their families, spent time together when not working. The two men became firm friends and enjoyed many-a-late-night sipping Scotch and discussing all-things football. In addition they would run, play tennis or squash together and, despite being ten years his junior, Crosby struggled to keep up with Geordie's pace. The younger coach was also continually picking the brain of new mentor, with Geordie more than willing to share and advise.

However, in the summer of 1987, Crosby and his family were resigned to heading home – but this is when his new friend stepped in. Geordie had been offered a new challenge at Salmiya, another Kuwaiti top flight side, but one who had finished second to bottom in 1986 and 1987. Armstrong had accepted the role and recommended Malcolm Crosby should be interviewed as Youth Team coach – Crosby recognises that Geordie no doubt had a big say in him getting the role and he and his family were delighted to be staying.

Crosby's under-18s won their league that season but, looking back, he remembers clearly working with Geordie and the first team most days too, and how he learned from his friend.

"I was impressed by his commitment, knowledge and the manner in which he treated his players. They had great respect for his coaching and of him as a person. Geordie was such a great coach, one who didn't have to simply rely on just explaining verbally – he could, and would, always demonstrate himself." Crosby continues; "He was just so encouraging and giving of his time, but above all, time working in the company of Geordie was fun, both as a colleague and for his players." However, he also highlights what has become a constant theme with Geordie as a coach; "He always reiterated that if you aren't prepared to work to be a good player, the chances are you won't become one!"

"After coaching the Al Salimiya youth team I would then bring my sons, Ian (6) and Neil (3) to watch George training with the first team. They would collect the balls and play football, but what they really looked forward to was

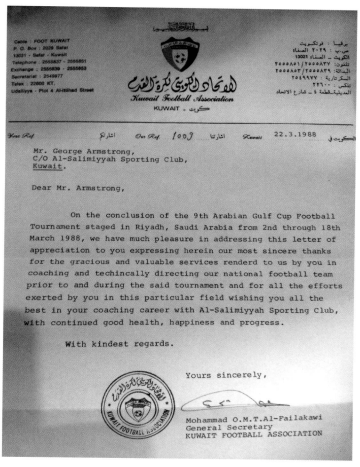

[Left]
Geordie was mentor to Malcolm Crosby

[Right]
Thanks and good luck from the Kuwait Football Association

the ice-cold Vimto after training, which the ground staff had prepared for the players and staff. They always came home mouths all purple after their Vimto.

One evening George asked me to go to the changing room to collect some bibs and, as I walked in, a member of the ground staff was stirring the Vimto and ice into a big tub, the only problem was, that he was using the handle of the rubber-bladed mop that he used to wash down the toilet floor with! George and I found it hilarious, but that was end of the Vimto for the kids!"

Crosby watched Geordie transform the playing staff at Salmiya first-hand and marvelled at how he instilled a new belief in the squad – without ever once needing to shout – just by using encouragement, patience and hard work, Crosby comments; "I certainly became a better coach working along-side Geordie and learned plenty from his experience both as a top player and coach." By the end of the season Salmiya had moved from second bottom to finish third, just three points off the top. Crosby was then offered the role of assistant to Dennis Smith, his old boss at York, who had taken over as man-ager at Sunderland – it was obviously an offer he had to accept.

In 1992 Crosby was given the manager's position at Sunderland and recalls; "It gave me a chance to show my appreciation to George by asking him to be my first-team coach and assistant, but by that stage, he was coaching at Arsenal and decided to stay at the club he felt was home. To this day I am convinced that, had he joined me, I would have been successful a lot longer with Gerodie at that club with me."

But just before Crosby's departure, in the February of 1988, he had witnessed the Kuwaiti FA come to Geordie, while Salmiya were riding high, to ask if he would once more step into coach the national team for the Gulf Cup that March. Brazilian, Antonio Vieira, had been relieved of his duties having lost at home to Tunisia and Egypt in the previous Autumn and it was Armstrong who they'd turned to, and who obliged.

Geordie's first game in temporary charge saw Kuwait win 3-0 against European opposition in the shape of Czechoslovakia, before taking the team to Saudi Arabia for the Gulf Cup. Sadly, for Geordie, he was unable to repeat his feats of two years earlier, and his side finished fifth. However, his efforts were appreciated, as a letter from the General Secretary of the Kuwait FA confirms and he recieved a certificate of participation and a medal for managing Kuwait at the 1988 Gulf Cup, which are still with the family.

The wording translated reads: *This is a Certificate of Participation awarded to George Armstrong. This is for the 9th annual GCC cup which was hosted by Saudi Arabia that went from 2 of March 1988 until the 18th of March.*

Crosby felt that Geordie was unfortunate not to be offered the job permanently at that point, but it was not to be so – Armstrong continued at Salmiya for two further seasons – 1988/89 and 1989/90. In the follow campaigns, however, Geordie was not able to repeat the early success at Salmiya finishing fifth and sixth respectively.

For those wondering at the level of football or the pedigree of coaches in the Kuwait League at that time, the manager of Al Qadsia in the last two seasons was none other than Luis Phillipe Scolari. In final season Armstrong's and Scolari's sides finished on the same points, one position apart. Scolari's reward was to be asked to coach the national team at the 1990 Gulf Cup, which he won, as Armstrong had four years earlier, whilst Geordie's was an ignominious sacking from Salmiya.

No matter how it ended, and the full details are not required in these pages, Geordie and his family departed later that year and flew home in dispute over a reneged contract just eight weeks before the Iraqi invasion and the resulting Gulf War. One again, there had been more highs than lows, and the family had enjoyed the experience in the main. It was a good time to be leaving.

Geordie landed back in London a little older and little wiser, but he was about to embark on a wonderful new chapter of his life – one that would see him reacquainted with many old friends and to opportunity to have a positive influence on the careers of so many more young players... Back at Arsenal!

THE HIGHBURY HOMECOMING

I t goes without saying that when his old team mate and friend, George Graham, invited Geordie back to his spiritual home to take charge of the reserves in 1990, it was because of his amazing character, combined with extensive experience and a winning mentality. However, those qualities would all be put to the test if he was to succeed in a role, that some consider, as the hardest at a professional club like Arsenal.

For a decade Geordie's side played in a Reserve Team Combination League – home and away against the reserves of all the other teams in the First Division – then, from 1992, the Premier League. Being the boss of the second string was a seriously challenging role, one in which the manager never knows from one training session to the next, or from match to match, the precise pool of players he would have to work with or select from and dealing with a combination of older professionals, mostly disgruntled at being out of the first team reckoning; younger professionals desperate to progress into the same first team; rehabilitating players on their way back to fitness and youth team players keen to move up to the reserves full time. Martin Keown went as far as to say to me; "If you were over 19 you did not want to be in the reserves unless you were on the way back from an injury."

To deal with such a fluid cross-section of players from week-to-week, and to do it successfully, required a special personality. Geordie Armstrong, it will not shock you to discover, was that man and held the post throughout the 1990s under Graham, Rioch, Houston and Wenger. But, as you will all know, very few footballers make the transition through the Arsenal Academy, to Youth, to Reserves, then into the first-team, but that is not to say that the numerous young players coached and encouraged by Geordie at Colney, or in his sides, did not make it as professional footballers elsewhere.

Breakthroughs at Arsenal happened more frequently earlier in his tenure, but by the later Nineties, under Wenger, the emphasis, driven by increasing pressure for club success, was greater. For a man as passionate and caring as Geordie, this was undoubtedly frustrating, but he never stopped trying to balance his desire to produce home grown talent for the first-team with a genuine empathy with his young charges and their aspirations to become professional footballers.

In this chapter I have spoken to many of the young players who came through the ranks at Arsenal and worked with Geordie for varying periods – some became household names and internationals, some did not – but most made careers in professional football and all owe a debt of gratitude to Geordie. Before that, though, who better to set the scene than the man who brought Geordie back into the fold at Arsenal, George Graham, and the person he inherited the Reserve Team job from, Stewart Houston?

Houston had finally called time on an illustrious playing career at the end of the 1985/86 season and, whilst considering his options, with the aim of embarking on a coaching career, George Graham, the newly appointed manager at Arsenal, invited him to train at Colney to help him stay fit and watch the coaching. Graham was then able to help his friend get an assistant's position to another ex-Arsenal coach, Dave Smith, down at Plymouth Argyle. Graham was thinking one step ahead however – he needed Houston to first prove his worth as a coach, which he knew he would, before inviting him back to North London. And that's exactly how events panned out – after help-

Determination personified

ing guide Plymouth to seventh in the second tier, Houston was offered the chance to take control of the Arsenal reserves. Then, in the summer of 1990 George Graham's assistant, Theo Foley, left to take the top job and North-ampton Town. Houston was promoted, thus creating the perfect opportunity for George Armstrong, who jumped at the opportunity to step into the role Houston had vacated.

So, was this just a job for an old pal? No, of course not, George Graham knew exactly what he was getting when he offered Geordie the role and Graham admits to having always admired football clubs that understood the impact of having 'club legends' involved in the coaching set up and felt it was crucial to maintain a connection with the club's past. So, who better to instil what it took, and what it meant, to play for the Arsenal in young professionals than a man who had played more times for them than anyone barring David O'Leary? Graham had earned his own stripes as Youth Team coach at Crystal Palace and QPR and clearly understood that solid youth foundations and inspirational football education is critical to the future suc-cess of any club. He'd also already inherited one ex-team mate, and another Gunners' Legend in Pat Rice, who was employed as a Youth Team coach, when he arrived – now he'd added another.

As Graham explains, to be a successful Reserve team boss; "It cannot be 'just a job' – your drive and enthusiasm needs to rub off on your players and, equally, if you don't put your heart and soul into it, they will pick that up too." Evidently the fact that Geordie was universally liked also helped no end. So that summer, a year after Arsenal's first title win in 18 years, George Graham had assembled a new team around him, a team that emulated the success of the side he and Geordie had played in, built on a collective team spirit and management ethos. The canny Scot feels that, in some cases, the managers get too much praise, however; "they also get too much individual criticism. It is a coaching team and every individual in the team has a key role to play in the success."

Despite having had three years at Arsenal by that stage, Houston recalls that Geordie took it upon himself to 'Arsenalify' his new colleague. "There was just no limit to his enthusiasm for the club and its history and tradition." Armstrong was steeped in the history of the club and he liked nothing more than to reminisce about old times, significant matches and past glories. In Houston he had found a willing listener. "There was just nothing that Geordie did not have a story about. A game would be mentioned and Geordie would instantly recall the score, who scored and when, and all important facets about the match. He would go on for five minutes and then look up to see his audience grinning at him, "What?" he would say, as if his elephant sized memory was totally normal." Houston always asked; "But how on Earth do you remember all that stuff?"

However, his story telling, despite including the most minute details, were never dull, and were invariably amusing – from Houston's perspective they were also very much appreciated. "Geordie was extremely quick-witted and sharp with the mickey-taking and banter, which are all essential ingredients to counter the tough demands of being a Reserve team boss at a big club." So how did the two men work together at Colney given that one was nominally with the first team and the other the reserves?

"Every Tuesday and Thursday afternoon we would take additional joint sessions. These were special sessions for a combined group of youngsters pushing for the first team, players returning from injury and first-teamers needing one-to-one work on particular aspects of their game that we'd identified." Houston reflects how much he enjoyed these sessions with Geordie...

"One of us would take the main group and the other would take individuals for what we called 'Topping Up'. It was this individual work on improving key skills for players on the periphery of the first-team that could be the difference between a player making it at Arsenal or not, and many players might look back thankfully for this extra attention, given when it was needed the most."

"Geordie was perfect for the job, his enthusiasm and passion were irresistible and infectious. He had a heart of gold and the ability to motivate to a level I'd not witnessed previously. He just wanted to help everybody to succeed at Arsenal but, if he could not see a way forward for a young player at Highbury, he would happily use his vast knowledge and numerous contacts to assist a player find a new challenge." As Houston confirmed, every player will find their appropriate level and Geordie would do what he could to smooth that process.

Houston felt that both Armstrong and Graham shared the same principles, no doubt partly born from the Bertie Mee era that moulded them as professionals, which instilled an ethos in which talent without hard work was pointless. Geordie practiced what he preached and there are many who are grateful to this day.

Let's start with those players who were in the Reserves when Geordie arrived to take up his post in the summer of 1990. Arsenal had of course won the title in 1989 in dramatic fashion but had, in truth, struggled to defend their title, eventually finishing in fourth a distant 15 points off the Champions, Liverpool. But were there any rough diamonds ready to be polished by the new Reserve team boss and likely to freshen up the first team?

History will demonstrate that the answer to that conundrum was an emphatic yes – the Gunners regaining the Division One title in a season that saw them lose just one of 38 games – with two young Guns having a key influence. Kevin Campbell played consistently in the second half of the campaign and David Hillier, having never even started a first team match previously, emerging as the midfield anchorman.

Geordie back at Arsenal and part of a winning team

KEVIN CAMPBELL – ARSENAL 1988-95

Campbell had been taken to Arsenal as very young lad and had stood with his father on the terraces at Highbury for several years before joining as a player, so when he once said that; "Sometimes there is just nothing better in life than being a Gooner," he was certainly well positioned to do so. "As a young boy I remember watching Geordie play. His energy and ability was amazing and he fully deserved hero status on the North Bank."

Kevin describes the thrill of meeting Geordie on his return to the club and how he instantly took to his new coach's infectious personality. "I admired Geordie's ability to laugh and joke but retain the complete respect of all the players." He recalls Geordie's special warm-up routine:

"He had a special run, along every line of the pitch, which we did virtually every day and he told us stories about how he used to do the same warm-up back in the day, that always got a reaction from the lads." Geordie, of course, did a lot of the runs with them. Campbell knew that, having tasted first team action the previous season, he had a good chance to establish himself further in 1990/91 – he was desperate to be ready to take his chance when it came – and Geordie ensured that he was. "He told me that if I wanted to make the first team I would have to work double-hard and I trusted him because he was already a legend in my eyes. He was kind, but tough, and I am certain Geordie helped propel me into the first team by making me work harder than I had ever worked before."

When the elevation seemed complete, Campbell thanked Geordie personally for all his efforts on his behalf; "We were sat in the changing room and he said to me; "Well done son, now nothing personal, but I don't want to see you with me for the rest of the year!" I laughed and said "I pray I'm not Geordie!" He just winked and started winding someone else up. He may have been small in size but he was big in stature – I loved him!"

DAVID HILLER – ARSENAL 1988–96

As far as David Hiller can recall, the moment Geordie arrived, his bubbly personality impacted everyone instantly. He describes how training was always fun with Geordie and how he used to use a drill that was unique to him that he called 'German.' "Basically on the pitch there were three teams. You had one team at each end and a team in the centre of the pitch. One team defending one box, another team defended the other box. The middle team had to attack one end and if they scored inside 10 minutes they could stay in middle and then attack the other end. The idea was to stay in the middle, but if you did stay there you would be tired out. Everyone talks about Geordie and 'German'. He called it that due to the likening of two trenches and the middle ground. Ask anyone who trained with him from that era what the first thing that comes into their minds drill-wise and they will say 'German'. "Oh no Geordie is going to do 'German'."

Despite his huge impact in his first season, Hillier was still in and out of the side for two seasons after Geordie arrived. He also worked with Geordie when coming back from injury. Hiller emphasised the difficulty of Geordie's job in dealing with unhappy first teamers, those desperate to get in the first team, want-away players and those returning from injury – as well as individuals who were simply not good enough. All coaches had their own way, but Geordie got what he wanted by being kind and non dictatorial. Hillier fondly remembers; "Because of Geordie's personality and enthusiasm alone you would do what he wanted."

Hiller is sure that the refined Wimbledon style of George Graham did not sit entirely comfortably with Geordie's beliefs, but he had to compromise as the whole club, at all levels, had to play the same. However, this being the case, Geordie was always looking to add variety to training and add his own style. Hillier called them 'Geordieisms'. 'German' was one, but he also added his own twist to the small-sided games where you had to score through a goal of small cones. Geordie went out and brought in a load of athletics hurdles and instead of rolling it into the cone goal to score you had to chip it through the square made up of the base and the top of the hurdle and then a team mate had to chip it back.

The club is only just, in David's view at least, beginning to realise that they might be losing the traditions of Arsenal FC. A few players come back but they don't visit the departments within the club. Geordie knew everybody and everyone knew him. At Highbury it was easy to go in and be personal as all the departments where close together. Hiller suggests Geordie's accent, that sounded like he was singing, was almost hypnotic and they all loved it. David says the staff now misses the personal touch and says none of the modern coaches or players come and chat with them. Now the club is employing more old players on media and TV side as they realise they are losing something.

For Hillier, Geordie's love the football and his club shone through at all times. He would do the whole session and if he did not feel he had done enough, he would go for a run. "Always full of beans was Geordie."

Hillier say he always cared about everyone he trained. He was brilliant, integrating new foreign players in the group. Lyderson, Limpar, Jonsson etc. Hillier is convinced that Geordie had a hand in a few moves of players away from Arsenal with a few kind words to other coaches and managers he knew in the game.

It was his caring nature that may have alienated himself, maybe from the top level or prevented himself progressing because he simply could not leave anything or anybody behind. Geordie could not do it because he had to be everybody's friend. But Hillier reflects "Geordie perhaps did not want to leave Arsenal and I understand that fully because sometimes you only realise you are an Arsenal man when you leave." If you ask any players who had left if they could come back on the same money they would.

David tells a story of when he was due to get a good run out for the reserves after injury ahead of a first team return, but he was in court for speeding. He had to be in court to try and keep license. He was not seen until 4pm and so by time he drove across London to Kingstonian for the reserves match v QPR, he did not arrive until 7.15. He apologised to Geordie, who said; "no worries it could not be helped, but you will be on the bench." Later in the week he was fined two week's wages but he knows it was not Geordie who told the club. Geordie tried to protect him, but one of the Arsenal scouts told George why David did not play as he was supposed to get a good run out on his return from injury. Geordie tried to look after him, which was the man through and through.

"There are not many people in football today like Geordie. Too many have a mercenary attitude but Geordie was the antithesis of that. Perhaps he spread himself too thin?" Hillier also went on to say that in the last three years coaching and managing in the non-league there are only three sessions he uses that replicate coaching sessions from his playing days. He uses not a single session used by Alan Ball or Terry Fenwick from his Portsmouth days and nothing from Ian Holloway at Bristol Rovers. He uses one George Graham session and two that were unique to Geordie Armstrong, 'German' and the Hurdles.

Enough said Dave – although in the modern world of football when the word legend is overused there is no doubting, for Hillier, that Geordie was one for Arsenal, but he also added; "If we're talking a legend of a gentleman, Geordie would be first on the list"

RAY PARLOUR - ARSENAL 1992-2004

Hot on the heels of Campbell and Hillier was a young lad from Barking who had joined Arsenal as a trainee a year before Geordie's return, but from 1990 to 1992, Ray Parlour was a permanent fixture in Armstrong's reserves. A year later, and at just 20 years of age, the much-loved forward had played in, and won in, two domestic cup finals. Parlour was arguably to become the finest home-grown talent of the decade and still holds the record for the most appearances by a player for Arsenal in the Premier League. Geordie would have rightfully been extremely proud.

Parlour in fact had lunch with Geordie on the fateful day and recalls him just being his usual old self – nobody could have had a clue what was about to happen. "Geordie often chose to sit with the players and have his lunch, rather than sit with the other coaches, and that day was no different. He was very much one of the lads and treated as one by the first team and the reserves. Geordie was able to retain the balance and was equally respected by everybody."

Rewind to 1990 and Parlour recalls Armstrong's arrival and that, without being told as such, there was awareness amongst the Reserves of what George Armstrong had done for Arsenal and his position in club folklore. "He worked us hard but we always trained with a smile on our face. In the two full years I had with Geordie we developed a real bond. We played cards, cribbage of course, on the coach to every away game." Parlour had been brought up with his 'old man' playing cards, so Geordie had found a cribbage soul mate, as he had with Peter Simpson and John Radford over 20 years earlier.

He also recalls the innovative and traditional mix that Geordie's training sessions provided, in which the 'German' gets another mention; "I assume he combined what he had learned as a player with the coaching techniques picked up abroad. He often spoke with me about his time in Norway and Kuwait with great fondness, the way of life and the other coaches he had worked with. I guess he must have been one of the earliest British success stories overseas?" Ironic, perhaps, that he also recollects how Geordie would often bemoan the fact that some of the foreign imports didn't like to work as hard as he would have liked?

Geordie would always join in to demonstrate what he wanted done in every session – whilst other coaches stayed on the sidelines; "He relished getting involved in any crossing or shooting drills and he was as you might expect – as accurate as anyone he was coaching. I have worked with a lot of coaches in my time as a footballer, but Geordie was right up there with the best of them."

Having been with him on the day he collapsed, Parlour vividly remembers the shock he felt, which was reflected amongst all the squads from youth to first team; "Geordie was just such a popular figure around the place. The fact that he was not first-team coach did not stop first-teamers seeking his company or advice and he was always happy to help, just as he always had time for me. His enthusiasm for the game, his players and the club will always be remembered."

Another unmistakable figure in Arsenal's triumphs in 1989 and 1991 is Perry Groves – a player who spent time as a senior player in Geordie's reserves from time to time, before leaving Highbury in 1992 – and another player fortunate enough to have played for the club he supported as a child. Not only had he watched Geordie from the terraces, but Perry's Uncle Vic had also played with Geordie from 1961 to 1964, so there was a particular understanding as to exactly why Geordie was held in such high esteem throughout the club – unlike some it would appear.

PERRY GROVES – ARSENAL 1986-93

For Groves, the memory that first came to mind when recalling the 're-arrival' of Geordie at Arsenal in 1990, was that most of the younger players had no clue that he was; "They simply did not grasp how much of a legend Geordie was at Arsenal and what he had achieved as a player with Arsenal. Of course the man himself would never brag about it or even talk about it."

Geordie quickly earned the respect of the younger hopefuls and disgruntled first teamers though; "All Geordie asked of any player was 100% effort and, if he got that, you had his respect and you were his friend. The respect was of course amplified with the younger players because Geordie was not a talker, he was a doer – he would show them how to do things as he still had the ability and fitness even then. He would never ask the players to ever do anything he couldn't do himself."

Groves reiterated that he was a very giving coach and he was there to support them; "If you wanted to stay on and do extra training or work on a particular aspect of your game, Geordie would always be willing to stay and help too. Not all coaches would do that, but come rain or shine, Geordie would be there. His enthusiasm and love for the game, and for the club, made him a legend in my eyes. He simply ate, slept and breathed football and Arsenal." Groves felt he and Geordie got on so well because of the shared love of Arsenal and because they were both wingers; "We both loved practising crossing in training and Geordie had lost none of his accuracy. He always gave everything on the pitch for the Arsenal, so it was an honour whenever he ask me to captain his team."

"Geordie seemed to consider everyone his equal, no matter who they were within the football club. He was a man of the people and I loved and respected him all the more for it. The two nicest people I ever met in football are sadly both no longer with us, David Rocastle and George Armstrong. They were both magnificent footballers but, first and foremost, they were also wonderful human beings."

ADRIAN CLARKE – ARSENAL 1993-97

Among the next wave of Gunners' hopefuls was Adrian Clarke, somebody who is also well known to many Arsenal fans for his passionate journalism and excellent broadcasts for Arsenal TV. However, Adrian is also extremely well qualified to talk about Geordie as Arsenal's Reserve coach as, from signing a professional contract in 1993, until leaving Arsenal for Southend in 1997, he probably played more matches for Armstrong than any young player.

Clarke describes Geordie as a very upbeat coach that liked to instil confidence into his players; "He'd always try and be a chirpy presence on the training pitch, putting on sessions that the players would have fun with. His characteristics were ideal for a reserve team boss, because he had lots of different characters to deal with."

"Some would be shy young kids, nervous at making the jump, others would be unhappy old pro's feeling thoroughly peeved at being asked to train with the 'bomb squad'. Geordie was a happy coach, he encouraged the players to get the most from their days with him. Geordie only seemed to get grumpy when he'd been lumbered with players who didn't want to respond to his positivity, which clearly frustrated him."

Clarke feels that Geordie was a hugely positive influence in his own career and knew that if he played or trained well, his coach would be sure to let him know, as he did with all his charges. "When you're eager to make an impression you can't ask for much more from a coach. His mantra with me was to get me feeling as confident as I could, because he knew I was a better footballer when I was in that frame of mind. He knew that positivity was the right button to press with me, so even if I was frustrated at not getting first-team recognition, he'd make me feel good about myself."

I was keen to discover if Geordie ever referenced his own achievements in the game as a coach, which I imagine could have been inspirational for some young players; "I've got to say there was no ego at all with Geordie, he was just about as normal a bloke as you'd find in football, and he hardly ever mentioned what he'd done as a player. In fact, I can hardly remember him ever boasting about his playing days."

Adrian's father, who had grown up as a Tottenham fan, had told him what a brilliant, nippy winger he was, which he recalls was still there for all to see in training sessions; "He had plenty of skill, and his energy was infectious, but from his attitude, you'd never have known he was one of Arsenal's greatest ever players. Geordie was a little bit anti-establishment too and I loved that about him."

Geordie had to replicate what the first-team manager did and, as Clarke remembers, he was often not that happy to do so. "If George Graham or Bruce Rioch played with five at the back, as they sometimes did, Geordie would mirror that in the Reserves but, left to his own devices, I know he was a 4-4-2 man. He loved encouraging the players to play at a high tempo, and use the width of the pitch, which was not surprising when you think that he was a busy winger himself."

Clarke fondly describes Geordie's style on the training pitch; "He wanted everything done with sharpness and in tight, confined areas to sharpen up skills. Small-sided box games were used almost every day. Some players didn't like it that much but Clarke himself thought it was brilliant. "We'd often play 2-v-2 in a really small area, where you could use players on the outside to bounce the ball off of. The aim of the game was to get the ball from one end to the other end, via short, sharp passes on the turn. His enthusiasm for this exercise was incredible! Every day would be like the first time we'd done it."

"Geordie also preferred 'doggies', where we'd sprint and turn, his sessions had so many races! The warm-ups often resembled kids' sessions, where you'd have teams of four or five – run to the line, do something with the ball, then sprint to the back of the queue. His coaching sessions could be summed up in one word 'fun', which was perfect, because it lifted demoralised players' spirits."

Clarke always found Geordie to be very approachable and suggests that; "None of the players would ever be afraid to go up to him and have a word, although I guess he had to play the diplomat with younger players and most likely tell a few white lies to pacify frustrated players, but he did it well. I sometimes shared a lift with Geordie to training when we would talk about anything." He relished the time spent chatting to his mentor about football, current news or whatever; "If I wanted to ask him something he'd give me a straight answer. He wasn't like a normal manager in that regard, he never made himself aloof."

While Clarke reiterated that his coach never bragged about his playing days with specifics, what did come through clearly was the sense of tradition and the expectations of being an Arsenal player that were instilled by Geordie; "In terms of his attitude towards the club he expected very high standards. He wanted us to look smart, behave in the right manner, and give it our best on the pitch. No matter what level you play at for Arsenal, from the under-10s to the first team, there was always a code of practice and standards that had to be maintained." Geordie was keen to ensure his squad all kept that up. "I think he'd get frustrated with the lack of opportunities some of his best young players had in the first team, and he'd make a point of telling us, but that aside, he was a proper club man."

Looking back, Clarke feels that it was Geordie's warmth as a man that stands out the most; "He always had time for people and made an effort to be cheery with them. He'd never have a problem carrying the bags of balls, bibs or cones himself. Some coaches would demand the kids get them in, and obviously he liked it if they helped, but I vividly remembers Geordie dragging bags across the training ground and never moaning about it."

In his five years at the club Clarke thinks he played well over 100 games for Geordie and that it was the coach's management style which brought out the best in him.

"Geordie knew that praising helped my game and, even if I had an off day, Geordie would resist slaughtering me and damage my confidence. In the youth team, Pat Rice had constantly told me to pass the ball, knowing that I wanted to dribble with it and take players on and Geordie gave me licence to run at defenders too – he wanted me to go past them and get lots of crosses into the box."

By allowing Clarke to play his natural game, he is convinced that Geordie helped him catch the eye of George Graham and Bruce Rioch. "Being positive got me my chance in the first team. Geordie helped me become more aggressive too and to not allow myself to be bullied, which held me in good stead in the lower leagues after I left Arsenal."

Clarke unreservedly describes Geordie as; "The nicest bloke in the world..." but laughs at his obsession with the 'f' word, which all the lads found hilarious. "In a football environment he'd swear with almost every other word without realising it. There was one match at Welling United in a pre-season friendly when the whole team decided to count his 'f words' at half-time for a laugh, and I am sure it was 50-plus by the time we went out for the second half! We started cracking up, not being able to contain ourselves, and I am pretty sure he clocked what we were doing. It was very funny." The irony is, of course, that Geordie would never, ever use the word at home in front of his family!

"I once picked Geordie up at his home in Abington, on the Sunday morning the clocks had gone forward. I knocked on his door, and waited and waited and waited. I then knocked louder. Eventually he came to the door in his pyjamas, hair sticking up, and sleepy eyes, saying "Fucking hell Clarkey you're a bit keen, aren't you son?!" I said "Geordie, its 9 am, not 8 am. The clocks have changed." And then he just burst into laughter, and dashed upstairs to get changed. I think he asked me to promise not to tell the lads!" Your secret is safe with us Clarkey!

JUSTIN LEE 1991-1999

Whilst Justin Lee never quite made the first-team at Arsenal, he played for Geordie in the reserves at left-back for many years and recalls how he virtually ran the reserves as his own little club within a club – from the organising of every session to even getting kit and balls ready – Geordie would be there earlier than all his players getting ready for the day ahead. For Lee, what was so special about Geordie, was that he treated every player exactly the same; "Whether you were a youngster approaching your first game or a disgruntled Paul Davis with over 300."

Lee's call-up from the Youth team came in an away game at Luton; "Geordie wanted me to feel totally at ease. He talked to the team, and to every player individually in a calm and relaxed fashion and always knew the right words. He was a humble man who just wanted the very best for every player he worked with and it came through every day."

"He was equally relaxed putting his arm around a senior player who wanted to be back in the first team as he was with a youngster like me who was just keen to progress. Everybody knew what Geordie had achieved for Arsenal, although he never talked about it, we all knew. His door, unlike that of some of the coaching staff, was always open and I know that it was not just reserve team players who would pop in for a chat."

Training was a mixture of old and new methods and firmly with a Geordie stamp, but one feature he had retained from his days as a player under Bertie Mee was something Lee referred to as 'The Board and Brick' or 'The Dreaded Car Park Run.' "This would involve a set up in the old Colney car park, where at each end a board was placed at an angle on a brick base. The players had to run full-pace, for either one or two minutes. Geordie would have the stop watch, but also be counting the sound the raised boards made when you had to spring off them on the turn... the noise ensured no cheating or short cuts were made. Suffice to say, it was not one of his most popular drills, but we all knew it was coming at least once a week."

Lee, who is now a coach himself, eventually left Arsenal to play at Watford, before spells at Bristol City and Oxford City, but looks back fondly at his time with Geordie Armstrong. Even though his career did not progress at Arsenal he was grateful to Geordie because; "Many of those he worked with would not ultimately succeed at the club, but Geordie was passionate about ensuring we would be ready to do so elsewhere."

In 1996, as we know, Arsene Wenger arrived, and with him, came many new overseas signings. Opportunities would become increasingly rare for Arsenal's home-grown youth development prospects and one of the last to break through from Geordie's squad before the Frenchman's arrival, and to survive into the new era, was a young Gun by the name of Stephen Hughes.

Most of the young professionals who broke through from Geordie's reserves will feel they owed him a debt of gratitude, but for some, he was a true mentor and friend too. Stephen Hughes won the Double under Wenger in 1998, but when he looks back at his time at the club he supported as a boy, Geordie is the person he thinks of first as a key influence.

His first experience of Geordie was as a 15-year-old boy whilst still at school – he'd not signed as a Youth team apprentice at that stage, but had been asked to play for the reserves. "There had been a letter from the club to my school requesting I should be allowed to leave early, so my dad could drive me to Loftus Road where I was to make my debut against QPR. I was a goofy teenager with too much gel in his hair, and I turned up in my school uniform and a tie." He muses that the like likes of Morrow and Merson, who were there and in the team, must have thought he was the tea boy. "Geordie spoke to me at length, tried to calm my nerves. Then, after a shocking performance where we lost 2-1, he hammered everyone else but praised me! It was typical of Geordie looking back, he knew exactly what he was doing. A young boy climbed back into his dad's car afterwards feeling ten feet tall and believing in his future as a professional footballer."

Hughes underlines how difficult it was to be the Reserves' boss and blend a team spirit from a mixed bag, but Geordie always managed by treating everyone in his charge as an individual and with understanding. "It was no mean feat to get hacked-off, out of favour first-teamers, to play at their optimum, but he always seemed to. His empathy was critical, but the fact that he was just so bubbly and infectious was also superb. You were never far from laughter when you trained with Geordie and we all wanted to work for him."

Hughes highlights the non-stop encouragement from Geordie as he pushed for his first-team breakthrough and how proud his mentor was when he made his debut in 1995/96. And even when Hughes had become more of a regular with the first-team during 1996/7, Geordie would still be on the phone to him in the evenings, "He would call with words of encouragement or congratulations." After initially playing fairly regularly under Wenger, Hughes found himself in and out of favour, but whenever he was feeling low, or back with the reserves; "Geordie was there, telling me about his faith in me and my ability as a player."

One significant incident stands out, which as far as Hughes is concerned, tells us everything about the man. In 1999, having played well for Wenger in the Premier League, Pat Rice had taken Hughes to one side on the eve of a match and informed him that he was not in the 16-man squad travelling to the next game and that he would be training with the reserves that afternoon instead. Hughes regrets it; "But I lost my head completely. I was so angry and disrupted Geordie's training session. I'm not proud of it, but in those

The Arsenal way: Geordie, Akers and Rice

days, being in the first team was everything." The following day someone, although not Geordie, must have reported his disruptive behaviour to Wenger as he was hit with a £1,000 fine that would be docked from his wages.

"Geordie should have been angry but he just took me for a cup of tea and spent 20 minutes trying to calm me down and telling me that I was better than that kind of behaviour – he told me that I needed to get my head down, work hard, and show them." He then told Hughes exactly what to do to make things right with Wenger and for the player himself.

"He suggested that I go straight to Arsene and tell him that rather than wait to be fined, that I would like to write a personal cheque to the then newly-launched Willow Foundation." He followed Geordie's advice, with the following results – "Wenger said it was a lovely and honourable thing to do, Bob Wilson was moved to tears and I felt good about myself again."

"Geordie knew all that would happen, because he was a people-person. Geordie was a genuinely unselfish and thorough thoughtful person. The truth is you don't meet that many in football as it is mostly a dog-eat-dog world. Geordie had a lovely way about him and he cared so much about his lads."

Nothing brought this home more to Hughes than when he was told he was not in Wenger's plans and that several clubs had expressed an interest. "As a Gunner through-and-through, to be told you are not wanted at Arsenal is difficult to bear."

Hughes found himself on a train to Liverpool to have a medical at Everton. Most of the tests were concluded on the first day, but there were some additional stuff to be done the morning after, ahead of an 11am press conference to unveil Hughes as a new signing.

"I was staying in the City and was invited by the club to attend a reserve team game. Having been unable to turn on my mobile all day and because the reception was so poor, it was only at half time at the game that I was able to listen to the five voicemails I had waiting.

One was from Geordie telling me what a great club Everton were, how well I would do there, how proud he was of me, and how I should feel free to call him anytime as he would always be there for me." Hughes was deeply moved and it brought a lump to his throat. Kevin Campbell, a close friend who had already signed for Everton, was there too and agreed it was so typical of the man Geordie was.

It is to Hughes' eternal regret that, despite playing voicemail tennis over the next few weeks, that he and Geordie never actually spoke again. He had called and thanked Geordie and Geordie had wished him the best for his Everton debut. Geordie then called to congratulate him on his first Everton goal and Hughes called back to say thanks and did he see it on *Match of the Day* – and so on.

Hughes was devastated when he heard the news of his mentor's tragic demise and both he and Kevin Campbell had to console each other when they found out they could not make the funeral because of playing commitments. The flowers that were there in his place read:

ALWAYS REMEMBERED WITH VERY SPECIAL MEMORIES.
YOU WILL BE GREATLY MISSED.
SPEPHEN HUGHES.

THE ARSENE WENGER YEARS

The arrival of Arsene Wenger in 1996, along with his right-hand man, Boro Primorac, surprisingly saw minimal changes early on – Stewart Houston departed, but Pat Rice and Geordie Armstrong retained their roles in the new regime. Rice had been in touch with Wenger prior to his arrival and, on Geordie's advice, had agreed to blood a certain Patrick Vieira before the French manager's Highbury start-date. For Geordie it was business as usual and, as the following letter to his family shortly after his passing shows, Wenger had grown to value the counsel of his Reserve team coach. I can only imagine how much of Arsenal's values and traditions were instilled in Wenger by the duo, but I could hazard an educated guess!

April 30, 2001

Dear Jill,
Mr. Wenger has written the enclosed words about your Dad and hopes they will be suitable for your 'Book of Memories'.
Geordie is still so greatly missed by me personally and I know all the players and staff out at the training ground. Take care.
Yours sincerely
Sheila, Mr. Wenger's secretary

George was a man full of energy with a genuine and honest attitude. He has contributed so much to the success of this club, first by playing, then by developing young players, that everybody at the club had the greatest respect for him. He was, as well, an open-minded man and many times we had conversations about different way of lives in other countries. He wanted always to become a better coach and opened discussions about how to improve players in different aspects of their game. He always liked to joke and that kept everybody happy in some difficult periods. I personally appreciated as well that part of his personality that showed that the 'winner' was as well a generous and sensitive person. Thanks George
Arsene Wenger

Breaking through into the first team became increasingly difficult for the young homegrown talent at Arsenal in the early Wenger years – the new regime bringing with it an influx of French flair and experience. But, despite this, Geordie continued to work hard to hone young professionals that were capable of pushing for a first-team place at Arsenal, or elsewhere, and improve those on the fringes. One such player, who famously made just one appearance under Wenger – a friendly match in which he was sent off inside a minute – was Jason Crowe. He went on to have a long and successful career away from Arsenal, but is still quick in paying tribute to his mentor, Geordie Armstrong.

JASON CROWE - ARSENAL 1996-99

Geordie had made Jason his Reserve team captain, which he describes as an overwhelming honour. "Geordie had done it to increase my confidence and to make me more of an extrovert on the pitch." Crowe knows that this greatly assisted his development as a man and a player and, even when more experienced senior professionals were in the Reserves, Geordie kept faith with him. "Training with Geordie was consistently high tempo and enjoyable, which must have been tricky when often there was only a small group. Geordie was strong-minded and always willing to tell people what he thought. The players always took it from Geordie because they knew it was honest and in their bests interests."

He fondly reminisces about Geordie's constant joke telling; "If I I'm honest they were usually poor, but the punch lines always ended with everyone in fits of laughter – laughs that could be heard halfway across the dining room – there was no mistaking whose laugh it was!"

Crowe admired the fact that Geordie was, in the main, a bubbly character. "He would ensure spirits were high even if he was low, which sometimes was the case. He did not necessarily share his frustrations but the young players knew they were there. On these days he would use one of his favourite expressions "Don't let them get you down, just keep going."

Many of the young players clearly took this advice as most made careers in football even if they had to leave Arsenal to progress – the ability to 'just keep going' is essential advice for a young pro according to as Jason; "That ability to keeping going, as a lot us did thanks to Geordie, is something we all owe him for."

To Jason Crowe, and many like him, Geordie was more than a coach; he was a mentor and a friend. The pair stayed in touch when he was sold to Portsmouth in 1999 and they spoke on the phone on a regular basis, in which they would chat about numerous topics, not just football, right up until Geordie's death – Crowe's words to the Armstrong family after Geordie's passing sum up that bond. "Geordie was a close friend of mine, always caring and honest and I shall miss our regular chats, even if they were at the crack of dawn on a Sunday morning. As the conversation would come to an end he would always say 'love to the family.' I'll never forget that Geordie accent."

One wonders how many other Reserve team coaches would stay in touch with so many young professionals after they'd left the club, having been released or sold by their boyhood clubs?

Crowe went on to play almost 400 games as a professional games for clubs including; Portsmouth, Leeds and Northampton, and back in 2000, he wrote that; "I owe the man a great deal and I will repay him in every way possible. I certainly intend to live his dreams. I thoroughly look forward to seeing him again one day, sharing a joke or two but, for now, he remains on my wall with some vivid memories. What a man!"

OMER RIZA – ARSENAL 1998–99

Omer Riza, who is currently Player/Manager at non-League Cheshunt, failed to break through at Arsenal, although he did play in the Football League with Cambridge United as well as enjoying many successful years in the Super League in Turkey. Riza, a striker who faced the ominous task of trying to make a first-team squad that featured Bergkamp, Anelka and Kanu, and knew the odds were stacked against him, but he recalls; "It was the likes of Diawara being brought in on a free from France that frustrated me the most. It was a tough time personally, but Geordie was always firmly in my corner."

Riza had signed a two-year Youth Training Scheme contract and played Youth football under Liam Brady, Don Howe, Don Given and Neil Banfield. In his second season he recalls getting his first call up for the Reserves on a cold winter's night. "George Armstrong needed a striker on the bench and, as I had been scoring regularly, that was me."

Omer came on from the bench and recalls that Geordie had a way of making players feel relaxed and were capable of performing at the level expected. No specific instructions, just go out and play... show us what you can do. "Geordie was never concerned who you were, if you were with his reserves, whether as a regular, a youth lad playing up a level, a frustrated first-teamer or somebody returning from injury. You were his player."

It was Omer's first experience of one of Geordie's end of match team-talks, and it is one he has never forgotten. Not because of the expletive-packed emphasis, but because Geordie told all the senior players that he wished he had played Omer from the start. "This was Geordie's way of giving me a huge boost in my self belief without actually speaking directly to me – it was a method he used often."

At the end of that season eight players were given professional contracts, including: Tommy Black, Julian Gray and Paulo Vernezza. Seven were offered two-year deals, but despite Riza scoring 27 goals and playing for Geordie's Reserves more than the others, his offer was for just one year. The news was delivered by Don Howe, Liam Brady and Neil Banfield, but Omer felt Geordie had not agreed with the decision.

"From then on I felt as if Geordie took me under his wing and I think Geordie was frustrated at the lack of first team opportunity for his lads. But Geordie still had a way of making everyone he coached feel at ease and positive about themselves. I instinctively knew that Geordie had my best interests at heart and my dad felt the same." After the first year, then a successful loan to Den Haag, Omer was offered another year-long deal at Arsenal, but Geordie encouraged Omer to sign for Gillingham instead.

"He always tried to balance his primary job, to make players ready for the first team at Arsenal, with looking after the individuals' best interests." Thierry Henry was arriving at the time so opportunities were set to become even more limited, but Omer opted for a move to Premier League rivals West Ham rather than taking Geordie's advice.

"Things didn't work out at Upton Park and, in hindsight, Geordie had perhaps been correct, but I never had the opportunity to tell him so, as just over a year later, I was at his funeral." Omer recalls feeling awful, however he is glad he attended; "I have nothing but happy memories of my limited time with Geordie, as well as a huge respect for the man. Looking back now, as I enter the early stages of my own coaching career, I realise how much I learned with Geordie. His training never seemed structured, but it was. It was always difficult for him as he never knew from one day to the next exactly who he would have in his sessions, but he always seemed to know when to be relaxed with us, when to be serious and when to put an arm around an individual's shoulder."

Riza recalls one Wednesday when all eight of the young pros had gone out for the night and had a few too many; "Geordie, of course, knew the signs and could smell the alcohol, but he said nothing and set up a shooting drill at the very start of the session. Everybody missing the goal with every shot. Geordie then sat us all down as a group and told us not let ourselves down again."

Geordie had the most infectious, loud laugh, which Omer says he will always recall with affection, but there were life lessons he passed on which have stayed with him through his career; "Lessons I feel have served me well as a player, as a person and will be invaluable as a coach or manager. Firstly, never boast, no matter what you have achieved, and treat everyone with respect and as an individual. You were never just a young player to Geordie; you were an important person, deserving equal respect to everyone else in the club. Geordie always had time for everybody at Arsenal – from Arsene Wenger to the cleaners and the canteen staff – who loved him." Omer recognised that and vowed from that young age that he too would treat everybody with respect. "Geordie was always loud and always laughing and if I was asked to describe him I would say infectious and respectful."

PAULO VERNAZZA – ARSENAL 1997-2000 & ANDREW DOUGLAS – ARSENAL YOUTH & RESERVES 1996-98

Despite their careers taking different paths, Vernazza and Douglas, as well as many others who played with the Arsenal Youth and Reserves teams in the late Nineties, have remained close friends. Both have now retired as players, but work together for a football agency. It is also immediately clear that throughout their playing careers in both League and non-League, the duo look back at their time with Geordie Armstrong with affection and, as I chatted to them together, with no little amusement.

With Geordie it was the simplicity with which he made his points and the natural ability to know what to say and when to say it. They recalled a classic Geordie moment together from 1998 that took place after training at Colney had concluded, on a day most of the boys had staying on to do extra work, shooting, crossing, or whatever they needed to work on. Gavin McGowan and Chris Kiwomya were working on free kicks, trying to bend or dip them over a wall of mannequins. Suddenly the pair started arguing, and within seconds, they were face-to-face and toe-to-toe. Geordie had seen it and had run over

A fitting tribute from Geordie's boys

to stick his short frame in between the two large protagonists. Having diffused the situation, Armstrong looked to establish why the friends had been arguing, and when he discovered it was over the technique of taking the free-kick, he turned the negative energy into a positive with humour as only he could. By that stage the rest of us had moved close enough to hear; "For fuck's sake you, just put the ball down, look the guy in the wall straight in the eye, then smash the ball straight at his fuckin' face. No one wants to take a ball in the mush!" With that he proceeded to stick the ball down and smashed it straight in the top corner of the net, then ran around the players celebrating as if he had scored the winning goal in the Cup Final. The whole squad were on the floor laughing – Kiwomya and McGowan included." This is another example of how Geordie used impromptu humour to diffuse awkward situation, but he would also use it in more premeditated ways to relax his players as Douglas described.

"I was making my first ever start for the Reserves, and Geordie, after being promoted from the Youth side – I was to play up front with none other than

Dennis Bergkamp who was returning from injury. In the changing room before kick-off, I watched Geordie go round to each player, one at a time, and give each a few words of advice and encouragement. When he got to me he said, 'Make sure your movement is good, make those runs in behind and your team mates will find you – and make sure your first touch is good.' Next he moved to Bergkamp, and in an exaggerated fashion, made out as if he was about to launch into a stream of advice for Dennis, then pretended to notice who it was in front of him before moving to the next player. In hindsight it was, of course, wonderfully staged between Geordie and perhaps Bergkamp, but all I know is that I ran out relaxed and feeling ready, still smiling at Geordie's comedic theatrics!"

Whether consciously, or otherwise, Armstrong always knew how to relax his players and make them ready. Both Vernazza and Douglas wanted to train and play for Geordie. "When you were at Arsenal you would always do exactly what your coach asked you to do. It was how you were brought up at the club and respect was taught from an early age." However, both reveal there were other coaches who they would work for because they had to, whereas, with Geordie, everybody just wanted to.

Both recall, again with amusement, how Geordie's sessions, though usually hard work, would usually end with a fun small-side game as a reward. "The humour lay in the running joke that Geordie would continuously change the rules as it suited him and to ensure that it was his team that won. It was part of the charm of his sessions and always guaranteed training ended on a high. It would be two-touches only, but Geordie always seemed to be allowed three – and the last goal was never the last goal until his team got it!"

Vernazza was particularly close to Geordie and knew he was pushing Wenger to give him game-time in the first team, but on the day Geordie collapsed, he was away with the England Under-21s and, after their training session, noticed he'd missed several calls. "I finally spoke to Greg Lincoln, who had been there when Geordie collapsed and I just went cold and numb when I found out what had happened."

Vernazza played for the Arsenal first team in the Worthington Cup the next day and recalls the minute's silence where the team held hands on the pitch, with Geordie's image on the big screens; "I remember looking around and there were so many of us, lads who had been with Geordie, all thinking he would have been proud of us." In fact on that night, not even 24 hours after Geordie had passed away, the Arsenal team included; Vernazza, Cole, Weston, Pennant, Volz and Barrett in the starting line up, with Mendez and Cannovile coming on from the bench. Eight of Geordie's boys. I am sure looking down he would indeed have been proud.

Vernazza and Douglas both look back and remember how much quieter Colney was without Geordie there and agree they had lost a mentor and a coach who they believed in, and one who had believed in them.

Lincoln may not have made the first team at Arsenal but the 'Arsenal Education' he received from the age of nine, to when he left at 21, stayed with him – now he is back at Arsenal as a full-time coach – instilling the same values into the next generations as George Armstrong did with him.

During the 1989/90 season, Lincoln was being coached in the evenings at the JVC centre, along with the likes of Paulo Vernazza, Julian Gray and Ashley Cole, and he recalls his first impression of Arsenal and the centre's set-up was from Geordie. At the end of his first session Armstrong took him to one side and said; "You are small, nippy and skilful lad, does your dad play as you must have got that ability from somewhere? I left that evening he feeling six feet tall. That little quip cost him nothing, but it meant the world to me."

Lincoln was also on the training pitch with Geordie on the fateful day and recalls; "One minute he was flying down the wing crossing the ball and the next he collapsed." Understandably he preferred to remember the great man in happy times and, to this day, Lincoln feels that Geordie was; "the embodiment of the Arsenal Way." But what does this mean?

"It is a way of conducting yourself in the football world both on and off the pitch and Geordie passed it down from his generation to the next. On the pitch it was about football intelligence and a thought process that kept you ahead of the game alongside technique and skill and the ability to know what you want to do when you received the ball. Off the pitch it is about respect for your coaches your colleagues and those you interacted with from other clubs because you were representing 'The Arsenal'."

That is what Geordie ingrained in them as youngsters of nine and ten and again, later, when Lincoln was a Youth player, playing and training often with Armstrong's Reserves. Ultimately Geordie understood then, as Lincoln does now, that Arsenal Football Club have a responsibility to develop not only footballers ready to succeed at Arsenal, but if not at Arsenal, then elsewhere. There is a commitment to develop well-rounded, respectful young men. Last year Lincoln managed an Arsenal Under-12s team to victory in the 'Truce Games', a tournament that combined football with a wider education experience centred on the First World War. Lincoln said after the victory:

"It is important for the boys to know that at our football club, we like to develop them as people. We know they're not all going to play for our first team, but we like to think that, whatever happens to them in their football journey, they leave us not only as a better footballer, but as a better person as well."

Geordie always had the time for all the players he coached, whether the seniors, or kids like Lincoln; "He treated everyone as equals and therefore deserving of his time and attention. For those who were being released and leaving Arsenal he would be on hand to put and arm around them and give them advice of contacts of his in the football world." Sadly, when Lincoln was released in 2001, Armstrong was not on hand, and reflects; "When you step away you realise how lucky I was from the age of nine to 21 to have such a privileged upbringing in football at Arsenal and Geordie was the biggest part of that."

When asked for examples, Lincoln casts his mind back to his first-ever game for Arsenal as 16-year-old, in the Summer Junior Floodlit Cup against Swindon. "I got totally caught up with the magnitude of it all and totally under performed. I was hauled off at half-time and was distraught. Geordie was not the manager that night, but he sought me out and took me to one side and gave me advice that stayed with me throughout my career. One sentence that I still use to this day. I can still see Geordie uttering the words; 'Play the game not the occasion.'"

Eight years later, and four years after Geordie left us, Lincoln was in the centre of Northampton Town's midfield lining up to take on Manchester United in the FA Cup Fourth Round. The opposition included a midfield that featured Scholes, Butt, Fletcher and Bellion, with Ronaldo and Forlan in attack, and whilst many of his Northampton teammates were in the changing room discussing whose shirt they wanted after the game. Lincoln turned to his colleagues and repeated that exact advice; "Come on lads, we have to play the game, not the occasion!"

And these days, whenever I see the lads at Arsenal in international tournaments starring a little too long at the Real Madrid badge – my advice to them is the same."

ASHLEY COLE – ARSENAL 1998–2006

If you were to talk to Jill Armstrong about the player who is most synonymous with the latter years of her father's time at Arsenal, without hesitation, she would say Ashley Cole; "He would be on the phone to dad most evenings asking for advice, reviewing what had gone well, or not so well, in training and always asking Geordie to apply pressure on Arsene Wenger to look at him for the first team." Cole was always hugely ambitious and determined, and when mixed with a tremendous work ethic and bundles of ability, then you have a combination that would ensure Geordie was always on his side. Just like Vernazza, Lincoln and Riza had done, Cole was first coached by Geordie as a nine-year-old. Those early impressions made a lasting impression on a future England star as the following extracts, taken from an interview Cole gave to 'The Arsenal Official Magazine' after the funeral, testify.

"I had trained with Geordie in the Reserve team since I was 16, but had known him years and had always looked up to him. He was always in my head, his words of wisdom. I still hear his voice on the training pitch. Every day I come into training and I still think I am going to see Geordie. He was a

Highbury Legend and a big loss to Arsenal, Geordie is irreplaceable."

Cole described training with Geordie as; "lively and always competitive as Geordie was still a winner. He would never want to be on the losing side in the five-a-sides and we would all rib him about it but, in reality, we loved that he could still join in training and make it so enjoyable." That, for Cole, had been the case since day one.

"I joined Arsenal as a nine-year-old and I would come home from school with a huge smile on my face knowing I was off to training. I owe so much of what I have achieved to him. He was honest and critical without ever being negative."

Geordie had applied huge pressure on Wenger to give Cole his break and the League debut finally came right at the end of the 1999/00 season, however, in the September of 2000, Cole played away at Bradford and scored Arsenal's only goal in a 1-1 draw, after which Geordie was to nickname him 'Big Time'.

"It was Geordie's way of telling me to keep my feet on the ground, but I know he was delighted for me. He was like a father figure to a lot of us."

The next two first-team appearances for Cole came on October 25 and 28, the second of which was against Manchester City in a game in which he scored again. Sadly, just three days later, Cole's extremely proud tutor had died. "It was a real shock to the system, and it is hard for all the boys, but you just have to get on with it. He would have wanted it that way."

Cole was right – as I'm sure you'll agree having read people's recollections throughout this book – the young left-back must have known that Geordie was immensely proud of him too. Few people would argue, that when it comes to out-and-out success at Arsenal and beyond, Cole stands out as Geordie's finest protégé.

STEVE SIDWELL – ARSENAL 1999-2003

It is wholly appropriate to conclude this chapter with the recollections of a player who was not only at Arsenal's Colney training ground that fateful October day in 2000, but witness the tragic events first-hand. Sidwell feels he owes everything in his career to what he describes as his 'Arsenal Education', largely with Geordie, but regrets he was unable to make a first team appearance for the club before forging a successful, predominantly Premier League career, away from the Gunners.

When Geordie collapsed Sidwell was a first-year Youth player who had been training with Armstrong's Reserves, however, Steve's experience was particularly painful because he had known Geordie since just before his tenth birthday when he and his pal, Leon Britton, had been unearthed by Arsenal whilst playing for their Sunday League side, Colliers Wood.

"The first Monday night we all arrived at the JVC Centre after a tube trip with our parents and were greeted by Geordie." Obviously the boys did not recognize this kind man; "But afterwards my dad's first words were; 'Mate, George Armstrong was coaching you, how good is that?' My dad was not a Gunner, but he knew his football, and couldn't believe that a real football legend was coaching his nine-year-old."

Sidwell recalls the glee he and Leon shared when receiving the 'Vinnie Jones Soccer Hard Men' video for Christmas in 1992, then discovering the clip where their coach was completely taken out by Chelsea's Ron 'Chopper' Harris. "We couldn't wait to get back to training after the holidays to confront Geordie with this wonderful evidence and to ask if he had been scared of the 'Chopper'? We were surprised, but secret delighted, when he just grinned then clenched his fist in front of his face before saying; "Don't you worry boys, he came off on the wrong end of me a few times!"

When he left school, Steve signed a YTS contract with Arsenal, which saw him join the Youth team at Colney full time and, on occasion, he would play up a level with the Reserves where he was reunited with Geordie. He recalls that; "One pre-season we were all taken on a run by Geordie on a course that he used when he was a player at the old Colney. As we set off he told us that he was the record holder back in the day, but it was the height of summer, and the course was horribly overgrown with nettles and brambles – it took us across bridle paths and over fences for a good few miles. 'Fucking hell Geordie!' we all said, but as he was running alongside us, we were all ignored. Training was always stimulating and fun with Geordie and he always had a joke or a story."

Training was further enhanced by the fact that their coach never stood on the sidelines; "Geordie was forever in the thick of it, either feeding over crosses or wearing a bib taking part in one of the teams and interjecting to demonstrate a particular skill or improvement. He simply refused to put on boring sessions but also ensured those taking part would be happily exhausted by the end. Everybody at Arsenal loved him."

"When I closes my eyes, even today, I still see Geordie standing there on the training ground wearing a wringing-wet, baggy drill top – he always wore one way too big for him that hung down over his shorts. We'd all shout; "Geordie did they not have a top your size?" The wetter it got, the longer it seemed on little Geordie!" Sidwell wrote to Geordie's family five days after his passing and the extract below will leave you no doubt about how much he meant to the youngster.

"I would like to tell you how much of an inspiration Geordie was to me. I joined Arsenal at nine years old and Geordie was my very first coach and sadly, eight years later, I was training with him on that last day. I'd like you to know he wasn't in any pain when it happened and we did everything we could to help him. Geordie always gave me encouragement and has taught me

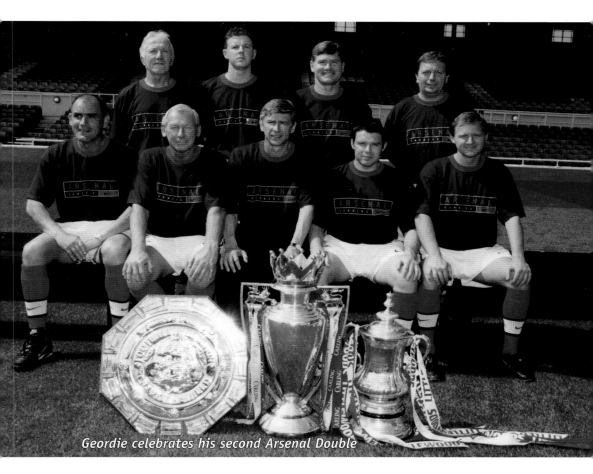

Geordie celebrates his second Arsenal Double

to believe in myself. He was my mentor and I feel privileged to have known such a wonderful man. One thing he always said to me was; "Be hard, but be fair" and I shall always remember that. I will truly miss him and never ever forget him."

LIAM BRADY – HEAD OF YOUTH DEVELOPMENT 1996 – 2014

When Brady returned to Arsenal in 1996 he recalls that; "Geordie was still Geordie, he was still as fit as a fiddle and could run longer and quicker than some of the players he was coaching. He always finished his training with a small-sided game and could be seen flying around the pitch with his players." Things had changed under Wenger and the Reserve team was not as strong – any player who was in, or close to, the first-team squad trained with Arsene – which Liam imagines, he found very different to the George Graham days, as he was a manager who actively used the Reserves.

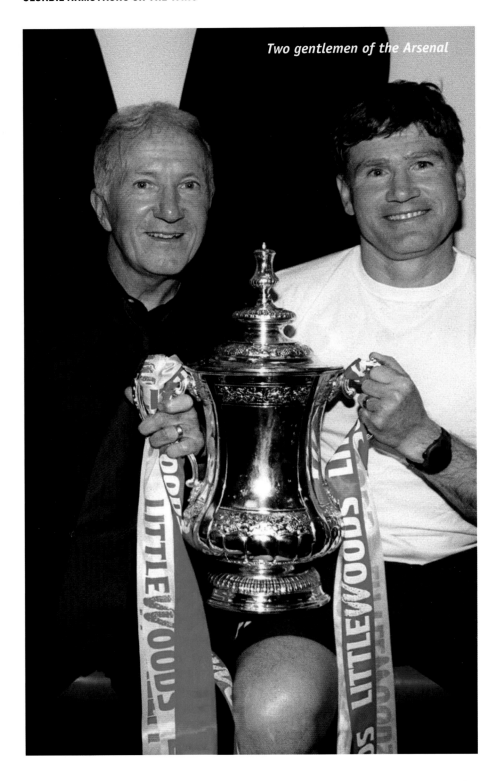

Two gentlemen of the Arsenal

Brady suggests that Geordie probably felt he deserved a chance to work with the first-team too, but it never happened. "Regardless, he never let his disappointment reflect in his work with his players, or doing his best for the Arsenal. Geordie was just a great human being who had time for all those he trained. Geordie was unique in that respect."

Brady confirms that Geordie helped so many boys move on from Arsenal; "He had a great network in the game and he would pick up the phone for his boys. Nowadays they have agents who give them a load of spiel, but who are you going to listen to? An agent or George Armstrong? George Armstrong every time!"

In the early Nineties the younger players did not have agents so they would look to Geordie for career guidance; "He had a great relationship with his players. Not all could be told, but if they showed professionalism and wanted to train hard, they had a friend for life in Geordie."

PAT RICE - ARSENAL 1966-80 & 1984-2012

Having played with Geordie from the late-Sixties until he left the club in 1977, Rice was as delighted as anyone when George Graham brought his friend back to the club in 1990. In a letter to Jill, written shortly after his passing, Rice wrote;

"To work with Geordie after playing together was a joy. He was, for most of the time, bubbly and alive, especially if he was looking for the lottery money, or sad if one of 'his' boys was leaving to go and join another club. He always kept in touch with the boys and they all, just like ourselves, had the upmost respect for the man. Everyone knew that Geordie could moan for England and it was one of our high-points when we would wind him up."

"Nobody could say that he did not speak his mind, but you respected that, as you knew that he was not going behind your back. Over the years we have gone through so much together; winning cups and leagues, both as players and coaches. Jill, I can tell you that we still see him around the place even now. A GREAT man is sadly missed by us all."

Rice feels his friend was such an inspiration to so many young players at Arsenal in the ten years he worked with the first team hopefuls and also the younger talent in the academy. "Young players of all ages wanted to play for him, they loved his training sessions and had huge respect for him, as did the senior professionals. One of the things that always impressed the young players was that wherever they went, or whichever club they were visiting, everybody knew and respected Geordie Armstrong." Rice correctly predicted that; "What everyone will tell you is that the whole of the football world loved Geordie Armstrong and so many footballers, both retired and still playing, will owe a debt to him." You were 100% spot on Pat.

THE MEMORIAL STONE

Ashort time after George's funeral the family mentioned to Liam Brady that, perhaps, there should be a memorial service in London, as the original had taken place near the family home in Cambridge. Brady, as you will know by now, was exceptionally close to Geordie, so he not only took the idea on board, he came back with something far grander – a more fitting, permanent tribute to his former mentor, team mate and friend. Brady had initially taken the seed of a plan to club director, Richard Carr and, from that point onwards, it took very little time for the whole Board to give their backing and support.

During his years playing in Italy, Brady had witnessed many memorials to clubs' playing or coaching legends erected at training grounds, and he'd suggested a similar concept to the club. Brady recalls the idea being met with unanimous enthusiasm and marble had immediately been mentioned. "In no time, what had started as an innocent enquiry from the family was becoming something all together more special." It should not surprise any of us really, because when Arsenal Football Club decides to do something, they always seem to do it in style.

An engraved stone was to be ordered, which would be positioned at the side of the main pitch at Arsenal's training centre at London Colney, which, in turn, would be renamed, 'The George Armstrong Memorial Pitch'. I am sure the significance and location of the memorial will be lost on no-one reading this, but the developments had come as a genuine surprise to the Armstrong family, who felt a great sense of pride and what had been proposed by the club.

Once everything was in place, there was to be a short memorial event at which the stone would be unveiled and the pitch named – the family were consulted over who should attend, the invites were prepared and worded appropriately – from Mrs George Armstrong and Arsenal Football Club.

The ceremony took place on April 28, 2002 at 11am, with close family, friends, team mates and colleagues of Geordie's in attendance. Many of Geordie's 1971 colleagues were there too, with Bob McNab even flying over from the States for the occasion. Peter Hill-Wood, the Chairman, spoke on behalf of the club with Bob Wilson saying a few words on behalf of the players. It should be noted that he had to compete with an unexpected chattering in the background when he spoke – the young George Armstrong – born four months after the tragedy, but by that stage a vociferous 14-month-old toddler, wanted his say too! George Junior certainly made himself heard, which prompted Wilson to pause and joke; 'Will someone keep young Geordie quiet, he is just like his Grandad!'

Wilson looks back at the constant chatter coming from Baby George and recalls thinking at the time, "It was almost as if Geordie was there with them through his grandson." He needn't have worried about further interruptions, because a certain George Graham had decided to put a comforting arm around Tom's shoulder and this took Baby George's attention. Apparently he was very protective of his dad and kept trying to remove George Graham's hand from his shoulder, much to the ex Arsenal Manager's amusement. Obviously no one told young George that big Scottish George was fierce on the training ground and not to be messed with!

For Wilson, the whole occasion was painful and just brought it home to him again how much he missed his friend – the cold reality that nobody had been able to say their goodbyes seem to make dealing with his departure particularly difficult still. The unity of the 1971 team was still so strong – all of them would go out on a limb and would do anything for the others – but

Arsenal's lasting tribute to a legend

none more so than Geordie Armstrong – who in Wilson's mind was the most loved by the guys. "I always described us, the team, as the perfect jigsaw, but without Geordie there seemed more than one piece missing."

The first team squad and Arsene Wenger broke training to come and join the ceremony and pay their own respects to the memory of a man and his family. The photos that were taken on the day show Arsenal spanning two generations and, of course, the wonderful blend of two history-making, Double-winning squads as the ceremony took place just 12 days before the 2002 Premiership was to be settled at Old Trafford – where the first part of Wenger's second Double at Arsenal was secured that season.

Ray Parlour was one of the Double winners present that day and, at the time of Geordie's passing, was arguably the most successful Arsenal graduate from Armstrong's period in charge of the reserves. When Geordie returned to Arsenal, in the summer of 1990, Parlour was a promising 17-year-old youth team player who had only joined a year earlier. By 1992, after 18 months with Geordie, the cheeky lad from Essex was in the first-team, where he remain for 12 years. When Geordie passed away, Parlour had played over 320 games for the Arsenal first team and, to this day, no other player has played more game for the club in the Premier League. Parlour has no doubts about how much he owed to Geordie; "I was delighted and honoured to be there that morning for the unveiling of the George Armstrong Memorial Stone and pitch. Geordie will always be in my heart and in my memories of happy times at Arsenal. It is impossible to think of my Arsenal career and my achievements with thinking of him."

In addition to what was a fabulous tribute, Liam Brady and Vic Akers had arranged for two 1971 Yellow FA Cup Final replica shirts to be signed. Marj agreed with Vic that she thought of Geordie as a number 11, even though he had more often worn the number seven, and had asked for a shirt to be presented to Tom Armstrong for little George Armstrong.

However, Brady and Akers went a few stages further and the end result saw both Tom, for George Jnr., and Jill, for her future first-born (Jude), to be presented with the shirts in specially made frames, with clear glass on both sides. This was because the shirts had been signed twice – on the front by the players of the current squad and, on the back, signed by Geordie's history-making team mates from 1971. These were presented by Brady, who also made a short speech about his friend, before they all moved into the Training Centre where a buffet lunch was enjoyed by all.

It was magnificent day, which although proved extremely moving for the family and Geordie's friends, the end result was a fitting and lasting tribute to commemorate one of Arsenal's finest.

Each year since, on October 31, the family visit Colney and the Memorial Stone and are joined by those closest to Geordie who still working at the club, namely; Liam Brady, Vic Akers, David Court and Terry Murphy. A few words are spoken, memories are shared, flowers laid and individual moments of silent reflection observed.

One final thought that strikes me, as a supporter of Arsenal, is just how appropriate it feels that, for the last 12 years, and forever more, future Arsenal stars will break through to the first-team having trained on the 'George Armstrong Memorial Pitch'. Yes, it had been the same pitch on which his life had ended so prematurely, but he'd been doing the very thing that he loved most, once he could no longer play the game.

How many hours will Aaron Ramsey, Jack Wilshere, and Kieran Gibbs have spent working so hard to achieve their goal in life on the pitch where Geordie had trained and mentored the likes of Ray Parlour, Stephen Hughes, Ashley Cole and so many more? I hope they, along with the current young crop, come to realise the significance of Geordie Armstrong, and what he did for the young players striving to make it as professional footballers. Given the class of Arsenal and the education they receive, I have every confidence they will do.

LIVING WITH
A LEGEND

When I set out to write *Geordie Armstrong On The Wing* I knew it needed to be predominantly 'a football book' – Geordie was a great Arsenal player and a highly respected coach – so who better to assist me in convincing readers, if any needed it, than those who played with him, against him and who watched him? Similarly, for the years he spent as a coach, it made absolute sense to invite those who were coached by him, or alongside him, to capture the essence of Geordie on the training pitch. I hope I've achieved my objectives in those respects, but to truly know the man, it would have been remiss not to have a chapter solely dedicated to a few memories and anecdotes from those who knew him better than anyone. The words that follow are from his widow, Marj, and George's daughter and son, Jill and Tom – without whom this project would have seemed meaningless.

YOUNG LOVE

I met George on June 15, 1963, just after my 18th birthday. I'd had a falling out with a friend, so two girls at work asked if I would like to go to the dance with them to cheer me up. On one side of the dance hall, the Majestic Ballroom in South Shields, there was a bar, and on the other, there was a kiosk for tea, coffee and soft drinks.

George was stood by the tea and coffee on his own and the two girls I was with kept starring at him, so I said to leave him alone or he'd get embarrassed. So we went to dance and, after a while, George came over and asked me to dance. We had a few dances but he wasn't very good! After a bit he asked me if I would like and drink and I said yes, I'll have a cup of tea. George was quite shocked I think because he thought I would ask for an alcoholic drink.

He drove me home in his Reilly 1.5. He said to me later that if there had been a crack in the door I would have fallen through it as I sat so far away from him – in those days you wondered how young men with cars got their money!

Then we started seeing each other about three or four times a week and weekends. He told me he had just come back from Switzerland, but I still didn't probe any further as in those days I was very shy. We would talk about general things, but not private things.

Anyway, we had been going out about four weeks when my dad came in from the pub one Sunday and said; 'You know that young lad George you are seeing? He's only a bloody professional footballer and plays for Arsenal!' and I said 'And what's that?' You see I knew nothing of football. I worked all day and went to the youth club or dance in the evenings and that was my life.

Before that we had been out with my sister and brother-in-law and, as always, George insisted on paying for everyone. I found out later when my sister and I had gone to the ladies that my brother-in-law had confronted George; "You've got a car, you seem to always have money, are you for real?" George had replied; "I am genuine and you don't need to worry." But he hadn't revealed what he did for a living. That was George, even then, never flash or boastful.

He went off for pre-season and then we would see each other every six weeks or so. He would drive home to see me and then drive back overnight, sleeping in the car on the road-side on occasions to get back to Arsenal. After 15 months of this, in September 1964, I moved to London to live with an Aunt and to be near George.

Marj Armstrong

WEDDING BELLS

We got married on May 21, 1966. But it nearly didn't happen because I had booked the wedding when George was supposed to be away on an end of season tour to Turkey. Eventually he got permission from the club to miss the tour for our big day, but only George Eastham from the players was there.
Marj Armstrong

A FATHER'S PRIDE

Most of the people who followed football in Hebburn were Sunderland supporters, and in the 1964/65 season, the Black Cats had been promoted back to Division One. I would always go home when Arsenal played Newcastle or Sunderland and the first away fixture at Roker Park was the January 16, 1965. George had left the team hotel on the Friday to go and visit his family and his dad was really down. George had asked him what was wrong and he said he'd been getting a lot of stick at work all week. "They reckon you won't get past Cecil Irwin", who was the extremely popular Sunderland right back. George just said not to worry about it and let's just see what happens tomorrow. Of course Arsenal won 2-0 and Geordie had a blinder, so the next day Edward Armstrong put on his Sunday best, suit, collar and tie and went down to his local pub where most of his work-mates would be drinking. He walked to the bar, smiling, and head held high, rightly proud of his son.
Marj Armstrong

BEFORE WINNING THE TITLE AT WHITE HART LANE

My dad and I were making our way to White Hart Lane in a friend's car, but had to park up quite a way back because the traffic was horrendous and then walk to the ground. We were in the crowd making our way slowly when the team coach came past with the players on and Geordie spotted us. We managed to get the driver to stop the coach and we all hurriedly got on and closed the door, but with my dad shut outside. I was in a right panic as the coach began to move again, thinking my old dad would be left stranded as I had the match tickets. So I walked to the back of the back of the bus where George was sat and I said; "George I am worried about my dad." So George said; "right lads look out for the father-in-law". Someone shouted 'there he is' so the players opened the large emergency exit window at the back and George shouted to the Arsenal supporters; 'could you give us a hand lads and lift him up through the window?' The fans lifted him up and George and another team mate pulled him into the bus. Bertie Mee was at the front shouting "What is going on back there?" "Nothing boss!" came the reply.
Marj Armstrong

"Come on George,
its our wedding day!"

Geordie's two loves in life – football and his family

WAITING FOR DAD

When we came out of the ground there would always be a lot of supporters waiting for dad's autograph and he would sign each one, much to my, and my brother's, frustration. Dad, however, would continue to sign until he had done them all and we would wait. To be honest, dad was always wonderful and would always give his time to each and every supporter.

I think my first memories of Arsenal were always getting dressed up smartly for a game and my dad driving to Highbury. My mum, brother and I probably went to every home game that dad played in – which was a lot!

The supporters used to tap on the windows of the car but it never scared me – it was a normal weekly occurrence. They were always polite and respectful. I used to hang on to dad if he got a crowd around, where he would be asked to sign autographs – that's quite the norm when your dad was an Arsenal footballer!

We would go to our seats and watch the game; we were often around loyal supporters. Many, I am sure, did not know who we were, until they said anything about dad. Mum would jump to the defence of dad every time, and argue with them if she felt they were wrong. It was nothing bad, just football comments, however, I would get upset and mum would tell them off.

It was funny, my aunt would slowly sink deeper and deeper into her seat if she heard any supporter make a comment about dad, knowing mum would be on their case straight away. We would share this story many years later. The love and protection we had for dad was there always.

After the game we would go to the tea-room. It was usually a long wait and often the tea ladies would be clearing the tables and stacking the chairs. Dad was always late and often the last one out. In the later years he was often with Liam Brady, both rolling in as the people were leaving. Tom and I never minded as we kept ourselves busy collecting autographs, which we did every game we went to at Highbury. I was very shy and would ask Tom to get mine, the usual "Can you sign this please for my sister too?" which was embarrassing, as I would be standing right next to him.

We got to know the old commissioners so well, lovely gentlemen. I remember one called Tommy, who could not believe how many autographs we collected, used to say; 'what do you do with all these signed programmes?' To be honest I have no idea what happened to them. Dad always signed them too so we would have all the team. It was a great time for us at Highbury, such happy memories.

At school we would trade football cards, but God help us if some kid had a Geordie Armstrong card, as they all knew Tom and I would want it. They took full advantage, so if we wanted it, we had to pay, and I mean pay! We would have to trade all our top players for our DAD! Another memory is of Tom and I going with dad to Highbury when he was having treatment by the club physio, Fred Street. Tom and I would get bored waiting around, so dad filled the big team bath up and we both got in and swam in it. I remember it being great fun and thinking it must be very naughty. I often have a smile on my face when I see photos posted on the social media of the players in the bath, knowing that we swam in it as kids.

Dad and I would go to St. Monica's church and we were always late... dad was late for everything other than for football – he would be early for that! We would creep quietly into the church trying not to be noticed, but one day we heard a child shout; "Look there's Geordie Armstrong!" and the whole congregation turned round and look. So embarrassing!

Jill Armstrong

HAMMERS HAMMERED

I can only remember one game really well watching dad play. I know I went to most of the home games because I had to stand outside the player's tea room afterwards with Jill and get autographs on the back of the programme. I used to get Jill's too because she was always too shy to ask. The game I remember was in 1976, against West Ham at Highbury. I would have been six years old I think, but I remember we won 6-1 and dad scored a great goal – I also remember Alan Ball scored and missed a penalty."

Tom Armstrong

FROM LEICESTER TO NORWAY

I don't remember watching any games with dad playing for Leicester, but that was when I first started playing for my school. We had lost our first game, before dad took over running the school team. I kept complaining to mum that dad was always too hard on me and I didn't like it. However, we went on to win the league under dad's coaching and I was top scorer!

Tom Armstrong

TOP OF THE POPS

We had been to watch one of Leicester's Cup matches and afterwards were having a drink in the pub. Dad had disappeared off, chatting to someone, which was a regular occurrence, when he shouted; "Jill, come over here, there is someone I would like you to meet!"

I walked over only to see dad talking to Dave Bartram, who was my favourite singer in Showaddywaddy, who were such a popular band then. I felt so uncomfortable, I was only a young girl and I could not speak. Dad never ever felt intimidated by anyone, he saw everyone the same and never judged anyone in advance, which to me, was one of his best qualities.

Jill Armstrong

HOOK LINE AND SINKER

I went fishing at the local pier in Norway, using a rod and two hooks that I'd found in the basement of our rented house – I had been there for an hour or so when dad turned up. "Let me show you how to do it..." he said before casting the line off from the pier, which straight away got hooked up on something below the surface. After some tugging and pulling the line broke and we lost the hook on the end, so we fitted the second. I remember he cast off again and exactly the same thing happened. I think that was the last time we went fishing together! Norway had a great set up in terms of youth to seniors. Whilst dad was playing over there I remember one game when a shot of his knocked out one of the opposition's players, he said he'd hit it so hard that you could read the ball manufacturer's name on the guy's forehead. In the same game Mjølner won a free-kick about five yards inside from the corner flag and the crowd were shouting "Banana kick! Banana kick!" Dad duly obliged and dispatched the free-kick into the top corner of the net.
Tom Armstrong

A DOG CALLED PIKE

In Norway dad would drive around with 'George Armstrong – Mjølner' on the side of our car *[pictured above]*, which was part of a sponsorship deal. People would honk their horn – it felt weird to begin with – but when we realised why they did it we thought it was a lovely gesture. Norway was a great time for us as a family. The television was terrible, so we did lots of

things together. Jack Anderson bought us a dog that we named Pike, which means girl in Norwegian. We also walked and climbed the mountains behind where we lived – as a family they was our happiest times together.
Jill Armstrong

KUWAITI ADVENTURE

When I was 16, dad got the job as first team coach in Kuwait with Malcolm Alison and two other coaches. I wasn't originally planning to go, but dad said come to Kuwait and you can train with the national team... What 16-year-old would turn that down? I went, but didn't kick a ball for eight months – it's not like nowadays when they have a friendly matches almost every month. It was so hot there that training was always in the evenings, so we had free time in the day. So, to keep fit, dad and I used to play tennis, which was something he was very good at. I remember him saying; "if you beat me I'll buy you a top of the range tennis racket." Most kids would probably have given up after the amount of times he beat me, but I had him out there every day playing. In the end I think he probably let me win to give him a rest!
Tom Armstrong

IN THE END

I worked in the local leisure centre near to where we lived and I remember the five-a side tournaments were really serious. I would get a team together and ask dad to play when he was in his early-50s – he was my wild card. It was funny as the older men were in awe of him, and the youngsters would think 'who's the old boy in the team?' But with the ball at his feet they couldn't get near him, banging in goals with both feet, then running back to tackle and block shots. Everyone loved him locally because he always had time for people.
Tom Armstrong

IN THE QUEUE

Just a short time before dad died, we were in a Tesco store in North London when a man behind us in the queue kept saying; "My God that is Geordie Armstrong!" Dad turned around and they started chatting about football and he signed an autograph for the man. Dad would stand forever signing and chatting about the game with anyone. That was who he was, and why he was so loved.
Jill Armstrong

George relaxing at home

MY BEST FRIEND TOO

To me, dad was just like any normal dad was. Yes he had a great job, but it wouldn't have mattered what he did, I would have been proud of him regardless. Everyone should make the most of their dads, no matter what, because one day he might not be there, just like mine. But he wasn't just my dad, he was my best friend too."
Tom Armstrong

My thanks to all the Armstrong family for their support and their candour. Your husband and father was a remarkable human being, and if any reader remains in any doubt about that, the final chapter will tackle that situation.

COLLEAGUES, FRIENDS & SENIOR PROFESSIONALS

Ihave endeavoured to take you on a journey through the life and career of one of Arsenal, and football's, finest servants using first-hand accounts of some of the most important people in Geordie's life, however, there are other individuals who don't fall conveniently into one of the period or category chapters, yet their thoughts and memories are amongst the most significant and insightful of all. The first example is Mr. Arsenal himself, and certainly not a bad way to open this chapter.

TONY ADAMS, ARSENAL CUP CAPTAIN 1987-2002

"I thought the world of Geordie Armstrong. I played under him on many occasions when I was coming back from injury and a more honest and enthusiastic man you could not have wished to meet. His knowledge of football and Arsenal was immense and I know that I, and so many others connected with the club, still miss him."

When Jill Armstrong first asked those who knew Geordie for memories, one of the early responses came from a certain Dutch first-teamer you just may remember. Rumour has it he could play a bit, well, Geordie thought so at least!

DENNIS BERGKAMP - ARSENAL 1995-2006

Jill, I was extremely saddened by the loss of your father, especially in the way that it happened, but I hope one positive to take from this was that he did not suffer.

In have known your dad for approximately five and a half years, and since my arrival at the club, he has always been very helpful, in fact he made me feel so very welcome from day one. He always had a story to tell about his playing or coaching career and you simply could not help yourself from sitting and listening to what he had to say. He taught me so much about Arsenal, the club's history and the English game, which for someone coming from abroad, was particularly helpful.

One thing is for sure, your dad played a great part in Arsenal's history and has left behind at the club many, many dear friends. My sincere condolences go out to you, your brother and mother and I hope that with all the amazing and happy memories you must have, you can all have a happy and healthy New Year.

The next contribution comes from a man with red and white coursing through his veins – the man who helped the club bring the likes of Dennis Bergkamp to Arsenal and, as it happens, Geordie back to the Arsenal too.

DAVID DEIN - ARSENAL VICE-CHAIRMAN 1983-2007

With 24 years unstinting service to the club that he loved, David Dein falls only slightly short of Geordie when it comes to service to the Arsenal. However, his relationship with George Armstrong originates a long time before he joined the Arsenal Board and predates even Geordie's arrival in North London.

Dein was born the year before Armstrong and has been watching from the stands at Highbury since the early Fifties – he recalls being about eight when he was first was taken to the shrine at which he has worshipped ever since and vividly remembers Geordie through the 1960s, when the player was busy earning his status as the firm fans favourite; "The Fairs Cup, followed by the domestic Double, were huge achievements for the team in 1970 and 1971, and Geordie Armstrong was essential to the way that team worked."

Years later, Dein reflects on the moment when the Board discussed the appointment of Geordie as the Reserve Team Manager – George Graham had put his name forward in the summer of 1990, which the former Vice-Chairman describes as one of the easiest decisions he can recall the Board ever reaching. "No discussion was required. Support was unanimous. It just went through with a nod, totally opposed." The reality was that if George Graham thought he was the right man for the job he probably was, but more than that, Armstrong was an Arsenal man and an Arsenal legend.

Dein often visited the training ground and witnessed Geordie in action; "He coached as he has played – with complete dedication. He was usually the first to arrive at the training ground and the last to leave. He would not stand shirkers and wanted his charges to work as hard as he did, but because of his manner and charisma, this was rarely an issue. Player wanted to train and work for him. If you had to use one word to describe Geordie it would be GENUINE. In a world of superstars, he had his feet firmly on the ground. A true professional. Everybody loved having Geordie around and everyone at the club respected him. He was infectious, and his bubbly personality lifted and motivated those who came into contact with him."

PETER HILL-WOOD – ARSENAL CHAIRMAN 1982-2013

The following message to the fans appeared in the match day programme on November 11, 2000, which was printed for Arsenal's match with Derby County and has been reproduced with the kind permission of the club.

"I knew George Armstrong for 40 years. He was undoubtedly one of the warmest characters that I have had the pleasure to come into contact with during my association with football.

Of course 'Geordie' was also one of the finest footballers that this great club has been privileged to call an Arsenal player. He was extremely talented and his talent was matched by his consistency – that led to him becoming the Club's record appearance maker – and a level of commitment that was second to none. As a player I am sure his gifts were underestimated and more international recognition should have been forthcoming.

Geordie's whole working life was dominated by his time at Highbury, even after his departure to end his playing career at Leicester and Stockport and an early coaching career that included work abroad in Norway and Kuwait, he returned to Highbury. He was very much an Arsenal man. His love of the club manifested itself in superb work with the reserve team over the past decade,

Friends in the Highbury tea room

showing the same commitment to the task as a coach as he had to playing the game. In addition to the many people who knew Geordie throughout the years, I'm sure the young players, who may have only come under his tutelage very recently, will also feel a deep sense of loss. He was such an instantly likeable character.

As last week's tragic news was being absorbed by everyone associated with the club – including you the supporters who had such a special relationship with Geordie – the sense of shock and sheer disbelief was a true indication of his immense popularity. George Armstrong was a wonderful man and, in every respect, he will be greatly missed."

LEE DIXON – ARSENAL 1988–2002

"A more passionate, honest, lovable man you could not wish to meet! When I conjure images in my mind of what being at Arsenal, and being an Arsenal player, was all about, I think back to George Graham when I signed – the Marble Halls, Herbert Chapman's bust, of Tony Adams, my captain and my friend – and of Geordie Armstrong in a tracksuit." After Dixon signed for the Gunners he began to learn more about the history and tradition of the club from reading and from talking to people. Geordie was always mentioned.

He also recalls watching tapes of Armstrong at his peak and he could see how difficult he would have been to play against. "When I was at Arsenal I would think ahead before each game and would have a plan in my mind for my opponent on the pitch. For some it was a simple as 'kick him in the first 10 minutes' or 'only show him the inside as he is one footed'."

"With some, however, the very best, it was hard to plan because they were so talented and were capable of the unexpected or had multiple options – players like Ryan Giggs. For those players you just had to be on your top game for 90 minutes, with full concentration and no rest until the final whistle. But I can firmly imagine that, in the late Sixties and early Seventies, for most right-backs, their nemesis would have been Geordie Armstrong"

On the occasions later in his Arsenal career, when nursing his knee, returning from injury, or when rested from the first-team duty, Dixon had the opportunity to watch Geordie at work first-hand and it was evident that; "Here was a guy who had a burning desire to make young players better."

Dixon also recalls that training with Geordie was a shock to the system; "His warm-ups, and sessions in general, were far more rigorous than those for the first-team squad." One can't help forming a picture of a coach who combined the best of the modern methods, with those he'd picked up from Mee, Sexton, Burtenshaw and Howe.

"Geordie was just so full of enthusiasm and full of life, quick-witted and always had a one-liner ready for you. He also liked a good moan, but never let that impact his work on the training pitch. As a senior player he didn't demand anything of you and often used the phrase, 'Be yourself and lend yourself to the session.' He expected the senior players to work hard and lead by example and he would use that example when speaking with his young players, either in training or in team-talks. He was inspirational."

Dixon wrote to the family shortly after Geordie passed away, which beautifully captures one of his special traits; "His character was infectious, it didn't matter what mood you were in yourself, Geordie had a knack of making your forget your own troubles by getting you to listen to his! I will always love him for that."

When Dixon played his final game for Arsenal, on the last day of the 2001/2 season at home to Everton, he brought down the curtain on an illustrious career with the Gunners that spanned 14 years and 619 appearances – if he'd played just three more games he would have overtaken Geordie Armstrong's total.

Dixon summarised how he felt at coming so close to Geordie's tally and, amazingly, it was a feeling or relief – he was respectfully pleased not to have overtaken him – just honoured to have been so close, which he summed up by saying; "You know what? I'll settle for being fourth behind Geordie Armstrong!"

Until now perhaps, it has been a little-known fact that Martin Keown feels that he owes Geordie Armstrong for his second chance at Arsenal. Having left Highbury in 1986 the defender was convinced that his long-term future lay away from North London after leaving on contractual principle, and it would undoubtedly have been easier for the Board had George Graham not asked them to ratify Keown's re-signing in 1993. It was Geordie who had been dispatched to watch Keown play for Everton on three separate occasions, and it was Geordie who had stuck his neck on the block and told Graham that Arsenal Football Club needed Martin Keown back in the fold. The last of those scouting games was to see Everton take on Wimbledon, a match in which Keown completely dominated John Fashanu – Geordie's mind was certain and he decided to persuade Graham to ask the board to approach Everton. As Keown puts it; "Geordie was an Arsenal man and I think he knew that I too was still an Arsenal man at heart."

Keown reiterates that he feels blessed in having second chance to meaningfully contribute to the club he loved thanks to George Graham, a factor that he shares with Geordie.

But things didn't go all Keown's way immediately when he re-signed in 1993 – the side were embroiled in successful cup runs in both domestic competitions – in which he was cup-tied. With Steve Bould out injured, and Andy Linighan and Tony Adams partnered in the centre of defence, George Graham was reluctant to disrupt the side. Subsequently, Keown was used in several positions rather than his preferred role and, on occasion, found himself training with Geordie's Reserves. During this period, when Keown had started to doubt his decision to return, Geordie was a constant support, continually encouraging him to have faith in is ability and telling him it would all come right in the end.

"Geordie knew that he had players who did not wanted to be there, but he used their experience to get the best from the senior professionals he had, getting them to assist him with the youngsters by using them as examples." Armstrong was also willing to listen to the ideas of the senior players and Keown recalls one such example when he was returning from injury later in his career. "Wenger had wanted me to get a run out in the Reserves to regain match fitness, so I suggested playing me as a holding midfielder, where I would get a better work-out instead of just sticking me at centre-back, where it would be too easy. Geordie accepted the suggestion and ran it past Wenger, who was happy."

Keown has little doubt that, by the end, Geordie was becoming frustrated with the changes in football and the diminishing value in his role; "He wanted players to fulfil their dreams as he had, and that in itself was fulfilling, but he was still a competitor and that was what he missed. I think Geordie missed the involvement with the first-team, which he still had under George Graham. He loved the banter and the camaraderie. I loved that Geordie would always come and eat his lunch with the first teamers and his lads at Colney rather than sit aloof with the rest of the coaching staff. But on match-days, or on official occasions, Geordie also loved the tradition of wearing his Arsenal blazer."

He recalls that, as a lad at Arsenal in the early 1980s, the huge success enjoyed by the 1971 team was correctly heralded and his generation grew up aware that the Double side had been the last truly great team in the club's history. "There was huge respect for George Graham and Geordie Armstrong and what they had been part of." Keown's favourite memory of the great man is a treasured moment that encapsulates Geordie so well.

"At the end of the 1998 FA Cup Final, when Arsenal's first League and FA Cup double since 1971 had been secured, I clearly remembers the emotion of the lap of honour and the adulation and reception from the fans. As the team approached the end of their circle of the pitch, and some players were going down the tunnel, I felt a tug from behind – it was Geordie. He said that I should stay with him on the pitch and not to rush off – explaining that he'd waited 27 years to be a part of something like that again, and that I shouldn't be in a hurry to leave that atmosphere behind. "Stay here with me and enjoy the moment, savour the applause and the achievement!" he said to me."

What he wanted his younger friend to do was to truly absorb what he had just been a part of; "He explained that once you leave the pitch, it is the final curtain falling, you cannot come back and you never know when you will next be here."

So Keown and Armstrong stayed together out there on the Wembley pitch, leaning against the goal-post, chatting and enjoying their special moment; "That special, evocative memory will be with me forever – I only wish some-one had captured it on film."

ANDY EXLEY, DEPUTY MANAGING EDITOR, ARSENAL FOOTBALL CLUB

"Its early September, 1999, my very first day at Arsenal Football Club and I'm nervous. I enter the Marble Halls after introducing myself to the commissionaire on the door – a commissionaire! The immense sense of his-tory and class is certainly not making the nerves go away; this is unlike any other football club in the world. My new boss immediately dispatches me to the UCL sports ground in London Colney, where the first team train. My first job as Publications Officer is to produce a commemorative brochure for the imminent opening of the new training ground, just a stone's throw from the UCL facility and I need to get the thoughts of senior players and staff about this very important development for the Club."

"I walk into the UCL canteen and there's Tony Adams, Dennis Bergkamp, Patrick Vieira and Arsène Wenger. Legends, which I now need to approach – and they haven't a clue who I am. The nerves of arriving at work that morning have now been increased tenfold, a pause in the chatter around the room and I swear everyone will hear my heart thumping against my ribcage. I recognise George Armstrong sitting at one of the tables. As reserve team manager – and one of Arsenal's greatest ever players – he's an important figure and on my list of targets: "Hello George," I mumble, "my name's Andy. Amanda [my boss] said I had to come and speak to you for the new training ground brochure..." I'm stopped in mid, stumbling flow: "Andy! Really good to meet you, of course you can, sit yourself down; can I get you a cup of tea or something?" I remember sitting down and kind of slumping into the chair as all my anxieties slid away while Geordie asked where I was from, where I'd worked before, which team I supported – and genuinely showed as much interest in me as if Arsène had just wandered over to him with our latest signing.

I'll never forget his welcome that day, how he turned my emotions upside down and how positively he made me feel about my new job and Arsenal Football Club. I know that I was one of many, many people on whom Geordie's natural warmth and kindness made an unforgettable impact."

FAISAL KASHMIRI (PAT CASH) – SPORTS AGENT, STRATA SPORTS

Geordie developed close links to Strata Sports after he finished playing. It was Strata that helped him gain the position initially in Kuwait and, later on, other short stints coaching around the globe. Faisal Kashmira, or Pat Cash to those who know him well, became a close personal friend to Geordie, indeed, he was one of those who rushed to the hospital to be there for Geordie and his family on the day he died.

Talking to him, it becomes blatantly obvious how much Cash misses his friend and, with his eyes welling up with tears, he told me how he tried to write a few words for this tribute. "Geordie was often in my office trying to help his young players find the right clubs after Arsenal had decided they would not be continuing with the Gunners – who else would go to such lengths? In my years as an agent it is probably only George who has cared so much. And who else had the front to go into the Manager's office on a Friday afternoon and demand to know why Jason Crowe, his Reserve team skipper, was not in the squad for a Cup game?" Pat knows that Geordie did and he would always fight for his players if they worked hard for him and he believed in them.

As Pat confirms; "The caring side of Geordie was there for all to see and he was forever talking about his family: Marj, Jill and Tom came first and foremost, but his club and players came a close second. On top that, he cared for everyone who cared about his Arsenal – that included every single fan. Going to a match in Geordie's company was a memorable experience every time because so many supporters would stop and say 'Alright Geordie?' or 'Are we going to win today Geordie?' He would respond with a smile and a few words to them all. He would light up our office and put a smile on everyone's face. That was the Geordie I knew, everybody loved him, and he was truly one of a kind!"

DAVE BARTRAM – LEAD SINGER OF SHOWADDYWADDY

"George Armstrong came from a generation of 'honest to goodness' professional footballers, untainted by the avaricious demands of modern commercialism, in an era where the beautiful game's exponents kept their feet firmly on the ground. I was privileged to share a beer with George after he scored the winner in a Cup tie against Hull City, whilst plying his trade in the late Seventies with my beloved Leicester City and it was clear his fellow pros looked up to a man not only renowned for his tireless efforts out on the wing, but the wealth of experience passed onto a host of young players aspiring to step into his boots. This account of Geordie's life has been a long time in coming, and I for one can't wait to feast my eyes upon it!"

GARY LEWIN – ARSENAL FIRST TEAM PHYSIO 1986-2008

For Gary Lewin October 31, 2000, will be a day etched in his memory forever. From being called to the pitch at Colney within minutes of Geordie collapsing, to administering CPR many times in an attempt to save Geordie, he was by his friend's side. Lewin also followed the ambulance to Hemel Hempstead Hospital in his own car knowing, in his heart of hearts, that the prognosis was bleak, but hoping he would stay alive long enough for Geordie's family to arrive to say their farewells. This is not the place for more detail, but Lewin takes huge solace in the fact that Marj, Tom and Jill all got to Geordie and were able to watch as the last rites were read and say their own goodbyes.

Lewin looks back at when Geordie returned to Arsenal and how different the club had become to the one he'd left. In 1990, even the top teams didn't automatically go out and buy 'ready made' replacements, most were still comfortable to promote from within – this was pre-Sky and before the influx of money changed the game. In the same way that George Graham was able to promote half a dozen or so Arsenal youngsters in 1986/87, courtesy of the work done by Terry Murphy and Steve Burtenshaw, he wanted to be able to continue to do so – hence the appointment of Geordie in the summer of 1990 was integral to Graham's future plans. Another factor to consider, in retrospect, is that the loan system was not used anywhere near as frequently as it is today – it was Geordie's job to ensure there were replacements ready to step up either temporarily or permanently, and Graham trusted him to prepare players for the next step, and to know when they were ready.

From Lewin's perspective; "It was a happy time and a very tight-run, small management group. If the reserves were not playing then Geordie would be in the first-team dugout. It was just George Graham, Stewart Houston, Steve Burtenshaw, Tony Donnelly, the kit man, Geordie, Pat Rice and myself. We were all friends and our families socialised. In the early Nineties there were about 70 people employed by the club, now there are over 500 just in Highbury House, everybody knew everybody, but they all knew Geordie very well. He would be buzzing around every day like he had a Duracell battery in him with his infectious enthusiasm."

"The only time Geordie could not hide his frustration was when players he was trying to improve failed to put in the appropriate effort. They were his lads and, if they worked for him, he would defend them to the hilt. But if they did not, Geordie simply did not understand it." Lewin also points out an important distinction about Geordie's coaching; "His player knew he was always coaching to improve them as players and not to improve his coaching. All his players knew that it was always about them. He was not looking to impress anyone with his coaching or to use his position for his own ends. With Geordie, it was always about the Arsenal, the football and his young players."

Towards the end, Lewin knew Geordie was increasingly frustrated that, for some of his young players, it had become more about the money and status, and Geordie would say to those youngsters; "Don't you realise you're at Arsenal for God's sake?"

Lewin laughs when he thinks of how well-loved Armstrong was in the world of football and how each new generation of players were surprised that, wherever they turned up to play, everyone at the opposing club wanted to seek out Geordie. "Is Geordie about?"... "Say hi to Geordie for me when you see him won't you..." The simple fact is that everyone in football knew him and, to many, he *was* Arsenal Football Club."

STEVE BURTENSHAW – ARSENAL COACH 1967-73 & 1986-96

Steve Burtenshaw spent many years at Arsenal in two spells, coaching Geordie and company during the initial glory days in the late Sixties and early Seventies, then later, as a colleague whilst on the coaching and scouting staff. It would be fair to say the two men were exceedingly good friends, indeed, Burtenshaw is Godfather to Jill's daughter, Mya, but their association began even earlier. Steve first met Geordie when he played for an International XI at Burtenshaw's testimonial game for Brighton and Hove Albion in November 1963. Geordie was just getting established at Arsenal and, just

like all the players that day, took no fee for playing, which was typical of players back then. Burtenshaw recalls saying to his teammates after the match; "The little lad Armstrong will be a star in the future." Little did he know just how much of a star.

Burtenshaw got to know Geordie much better, of course, after arriving at Arsenal in 1967, taken on as a coach to work with Mee and Howe. "From that day to this, I can honestly say I have never met a more hardworking man." A man who just appreciated the gift of being able to be financially reward for doing a job he loved. He went on to say; "Geordie was always the first in line for everything that needed to be done, gave his all in each and every session and was always on hand to encourage and advise anyone who was a bit down or needed advice. I can still see everyone fighting to be paired with Geordie whatever the session, but particularly anything that involved crossing – he was the first to be picked for every five or six-a-side game at the end of training – all his team mates knew what he brought to the team whether it was in training or on match days."

Burtenshaw remarks that he lost count of the amount of times he would over-hear opposition players or fans complaining along the lines of; "It's like playing against twelve men with that Armstrong playing against us!"

The other side to Geordie, that Burtenshaw witnessed on a daily basis, was his incredible consideration of those around him; "He was always there for anyone at the club who needed a chat, and arm around them or some advice, whether they were his young players or senior professionals. He knew when to give a rollicking as well, but only for the right reasons, more often than not you'd hear, 'try a little harder' or 'keep your chin up.' Countless times I heard him say to somebody who was down in the dumps, 'you'll see, it will turn out alright in the end' and, because of his efforts, it quite often did. Not many people, in my experience, had the capacity to do this as well as Geordie."

Burtenshaw is convinced, and we know he is right, that so many football-ers owe Geordie so much, and in 99% of those cases, they will never forget him; "I will always treasure my memories of coaching Geordie and watching him putting in memorable performances week after week – there was not a better or more honest footballer at that time." Indeed, he claims to be the man who coined the phrase suggesting that Geordie was; "The greatest English player never to play for England!"

Later on, as coaching colleagues, and as valued friends, the two men would spend many an afternoon chatting and putting the footballing world to rights; "He loved the game – loved it with a passion that you don't see too often these days." Burtenshaw and Armstrong continued their chats at least twice a week, even after Steve had left to join the staff at QPR; "Geordie was never afraid to voice his opinion and I often relied on his down to earth judgment, especially on players. I enjoyed our chats and I valued his opinions, but most of all, I just enjoyed talking and being with him, just being his friend."

VIC AKERS, OBE – ARSENAL 1984–2014

I'd like to finish this chapter with the thoughts of a man who'd become one of Geordie's closest friends – somebody who misses him every day. To some, Vick Akers will always been seen as the Arsenal Ladies' Manager, to others, the ever-present Arsenal first team Kit Manager, but to a person, he is known as being Arsenal though and through.

Born in Essex Road, Islington, a spit from Highbury, Ackers was first there on the North Bank on his father's shoulders from a very young age. Then, as a teenager with his mates, he had watched George Armstrong break into the first team, before marvelling at the ability of the man first-hand as a youth team full-back at Fulham – Ackers was delighted he did not have to mark Armstrong that day, and describes him as; "one of the best crossers of the ball in the history of football."

Ackers was playing for Cambridge United between 1971-75, but would be back to Highbury to watch his team whenever he could, so when Geordie returned to Highbury in 1990, Akers' initial reaction was; "it was a dream to be working with him." However, within weeks, it was apparent to both that a strong friendship was developing.

For Akers, "It was a bond built on similar personalities and passions. We both believed you should 'tell it like it is,' but only for the right reasons – for the good of Arsenal and the player involved."

They both cared passionately about their club and, if anything, for Akers, Geordie helped heighten that feeling. "We would spend hours together talking Arsenal, and football in general – Geordie was such a wonderful storyteller. I would defy anyone not to listen when Geordie began talking about an old match, or about old times, at the Arsenal. The senior players loved Geordie to hold court and Arsene Wenger enjoyed his tales of old Arsenal, Norway and his time in Kuwait."

In essence; "Geordie was always honest and true – two things there is not enough of in football. People in the game respected Geordie for his knowledge and his honesty."

Geordie was not only a great storyteller, but he was a wonderful listener too; "He was just as happy listening to others and offering advice and he was always on hand for a friend." Akers loved that Geordie always took an interest in the Arsenal Ladies and offered advice when Vic asked for it.

"It was what made him so special – he cared so much for all his players." And even when Geordie was frustrated toward the end and was left training a smaller group of younger players; "He looked after them all as if they were his own kids." Akers knows that Armstrong helped so many move on if they were not going to progress at the Arsenal; "He was forever on the phone to ex-players checking if they were okay, telling them he had seen them on TV, or reminding them they could call him anytime, even though they had left the club. It's was mark of his popularity that many of the young players who left for opportunities elsewhere kept in touch with Geordie and they felt they could talk to him and he could, and would, still be of help to them."

Akers knows that because Geordie had been a player at Arsenal, the club could never leave Geordie's system; "Arsenal was in his blood!" but also feels that because of the changes that had taken place to with the reserve team structure, and the changing face of football, perhaps Armstrong was starting to consider leaving if the right opportunity had been offered – Akers also knows that if that had happened, Geordie wanted him as his assistant. What a huge decision it would have been for two Arsenal men.

Akers still misses his friend so much and every year, on October 31, David Court, Terry Murphy and Liam Brady have a few moments by the George Armstrong Memorial Stone at Colney, when they say a few words to remember their dear friend.

On the day Geordie passed, Akers and Geordie had lunch together before Vic headed back to the stadium, he recalls talking to his friend about Geordie's son Tom's fiancé expecting their first child; "He was so looking forward to having grandchildren and he would have been a wonderful grandfather."

As this book is dedicated to the five grandchildren, who sadly never had the opportunity to grow up loving the man, it is appropriate to close this chapter, and indeed this book, with Vic Akers's beautiful and apt observation.

ACKNOWLEDGMENTS & CREDITS

I hope you've enjoyed the result of what has been an incredible and wonderful journey for this Arsenal fan, and I would like to thank those who I have met, and those who have helped me, along the way. First and foremost my thanks to Jill Armstrong, Geordie's daughter, for entrusting a novice writer with such a personal project. Without her enthusiasm, support and memories – and that of Geordie's wife Marj, and their son, Tom – none of this would have been possible or, indeed, as rewarding.

I would like to thank every single contributor for sharing their wonderful memories and for reliving their time spent with Geordie – the giving of their time has been hugely appreciated by the Armstrong family and myself and has been essential in helping capture the essence of the player, the coach and the man.

Although they have been credited throughout the book, unfortunately, space does not allow me to list everyone again here – but my particularly heartfelt appreciation has to be offered to Frank McLintock, Bob Wilson and Liam Brady, who have all supported me so much. Geordie and his family are blessed to have had such true and magnificent friends.

A big thank you to everybody at Arsenal Football Club for assisting me so willingly – Geordie would have been proud that his club was so keen to help ensure this book is such a positive collaboration.

Thanks also to my wife, Jo, and my family, for putting up with me continually disappearing into the study every evening for months on end, and for believing I had a book in me – even if it was all about the Arsenal! Lastly, my eternal gratitude to my publisher, editor, and now friend, David Lane, for guiding and mentoring me along the way.

Dave Seager

DEDICATIONS

The following list of people took advantage of the advanced purchase dedication offer, so their names would be included in the book, or were included as requested by a friend or family member who bought the book for them.

Stephen Cooper
Mel Oreilly
Peter Nelson
John Collisson
Danny Sweetman
Michael Clifford
Bish
Des Powell
Darren Epstein
Derek Black
Joseph Yarrow
Victor Hughes
Anthony Beasley
Richard Jones
Tony Link
Alex Link
Hannah Link
Bob Dersley
Raymond Cardew
Nat Goldstein
Gooner Del
Chris Moyle
Anna Lvova
Mark Horner
Dennis Skipp
Terry Conway
Ciaran McCormick
Bryan Anderson
Frederick John Willson
Tim Elgar
Sophie Jane Hollie Elgar
Charlie George Timothy Elgar
Penny Parkinson
Robert Simmonds
Dan Betts

Edward Grant
Jonathan Grant
Andrew Plumb
Mick Kilroe
Bryan Scholey
Janet Prager
Vincent Fabre
James Finneran
Katerina Sebastiane
Michael Green
Joe Kelly
Mark Seager
Pat Seager
Caleb Tatebe
Abhisar Gupta
Dennis Reed
John Hamilton
Lucas Pinks
Adem Murat
Jonathan Brooks
Amy Lewis
Terry Moriarty
Bob Hawkes
Andrew Milroy
Stephen Hadfield
Vince Smith-Hughes
Robert James Robertson
Tony Sharpstone
Nick Lee
Samuel Burton
Ginger Arsenal
Pete Doherty
Liam O'Brien
Craig Armstrong
Denis Bedford

Keeley Waters
Gary Lawrence
Magnús Pálsson
Stephen Edwards
Steve 'WINNIE' Winfield
Georgina Mullen nee
Armstrong (George's niece)
Ian Minto
Andrew Strouthous
Chris Grove
David Sells
Neil Page
Richard Sawyer
Mark Taverner
Steve Lowerson
Peter Turner
Mitchell Burman
David Hatcher
Dhruv Baid
Brian Hall
Matthew Hall
Colin Hall
Ann Simpson
Tony Church
Tom O'Donoghue
Keith Henderson
Jonathan Cousens
Gary Prince
Ally Prince
Judie Grant
Laurence Williams
Peter Antonioni
Andy Kelly
Mark Andrews

"GEORDIE, GEORDIE ARMSTRONG,
GEORDIE ARMSTRONG ON THE WING"